Cool Events at Home

Cool Events at Home

Stephanie von Pfuel

Carsten Sander (Photography)

teNeues

Cool Events at Home

Einleitung / Preface

Seit vielen Jahren lade ich gerne Freunde zu mir nach Hause ein. Es macht mir Freude, sie am Wochenende mit einem Abend- oder Mittagessen zu verwöhnen. Meistens kommen nur sechs bis acht Gäste. Bei Familienfeierlichkeiten oder Geburtstagen kann die Einladungsliste natürlich auch einmal länger werden.

Es macht mir Spaß, nicht nur ein gutes Essen zu planen, sondern auch den Tisch fantasievoll zu decken und zu dekorieren. Beides, Essen und Dekoration, ergeben dann ein "Gesamtkunstwerk", das für gute Stimmung sorgt und oft auch ein Gesprächsthema ist.

Bei jedem Essen sprechen mich meine Gäste auf die Tischdekoration an. Und Einige meinten, ich sollte doch darüber ein Buch schreiben. Diese Idee habe ich mit diesem Buch nun umgesetzt und verwirklicht.

Glauben Sie mir, man muss nicht viel Geld ausgeben. Mit dem richtigen Know-How, einer wohl durchdachten Organisation und einigen kleinen Tricks, die ich Ihnen auf den folgenden Seiten verrate, werden selbst einfache Einladungen zu coolen Events, an die Ihre Gäste noch lange zurückdenken werden.

For many years now I've been gladly inviting friends to my house. It gives me tremendous pleasure to be able to pamper them with lunch or an evening meal on the weekends. Mostly there are six to eight guests, although if we are celebrating a family occasion or a birthday then the guest list can be somewhat longer.

I not only enjoy planning a wonderful meal, but also decorating and setting the table in an imaginative way. The food and decoration often becomes a talking point, and helps create the right ambience.

Whenever I have guests they always ask me about my table decorations, and some of them have said I should write a book about how I create them. Now I've done just that and turned the idea into reality.

You have to believe me here, it doesn't have to cost a whole lot of money. The right knowledge combined with some organizational skills and a few neat little tricks, which I'll reveal to you in the following pages, can turn even simple lunch dates into cool events that will be long remembered by your guests.

Ich bin Perfektionistin, nicht zuletzt aus Zeitmangel. Deshalb plane ich möglichst detailliert und versuche bereits in den Tagen vor der Einladung so viel wie möglich zu erledigen. Jeder Handgriff, den ich vorher mache, lässt mir später mehr Zeit für meine Gäste.

Dekomaterialien, Sets, Tischtücher, Servietten, Kerzen und natürlich Getränke besorge ich einige Tage früher, Schnittblumen am Vortag der Einladung. Spezielle Zutaten für das Essen bestelle ich rechtzeitig vor, ebenso wie frisches Brot. Außerdem plane ich stets genügend Zeit für unvorhergesehene Dinge ein, die sich nie ganz vermeiden lassen.

Wie so oft im Leben sind es vermeintliche Kleinigkeiten, die letztendlich den Ausschlag geben und darüber entscheiden, ob die Gäste sich wohlfühlen. Wohlduftende Seifen, Gästehandtücher und gutes Toilettenpapier oder auch frische Blumen im Eingangsbereich vergisst man oft.

Ist alles gut vorbereitet, kann ich mich umziehen und schminken, bevor die Gäste kommen. Nichts ist unattraktiver als eine Gastgeberin, die ihren Gästen mit Lockenwicklern und im Bademantel die Türe öffnet.

I'm a perfectionist. Therefore I make the most detailed of plans and try to prepare in advance as much as possible in the days before the event. Anything that I can take care of beforehand leaves me more time to spend with my guests later.

Decorations, place settings, table cloths, napkins, candles, and drinks are attended to a few days ahead of time. Whereas flowers are only bought one day before. Special ingredients for the meal, as well as fresh bread, need to be ordered well in advance of the event. Additionally, I always factor in enough time for those unexpected incidents that often seem to occur.

Just as in real life, it is the seemingly small things that in the end tip the scales and make the guests feel comfortable. Things like pleasantly aromatic soaps, guest towels and good toilet paper or perhaps fresh flowers in the entrance hall are often forgotten about.

Then, when everything is prepared I have time to change and put on make-up before my guests arrive. There is nothing less attractive than a hostess opening the front door in her bath robe with her hair in curlers.

Immer wieder werde ich nach dem optimalen Zeitpunkt für Einladungen gefragt. Eigentlich gibt es eine ganz einfache Regel: Je wichtiger der Anlass, desto früher wird eingeladen. Bei einer Hochzeit, zu der auch Freunde aus weit entfernten Ländern kommen sollen, können das schon einige Monate sein, zu einem einfachen Lunch lade ich auch mal spontan einen Tag vorher ganz ungezwungen per SMS ein.

Die Anzahl der Gäste richtet sich natürlich auch nach den Räumlichkeiten. Ich lade lieber weniger, dafür aber interessantere Menschen ein. Dabei gehe ich nach Sympathie und achte nicht auf gesellschaftliche Stellung oder vermeintliche Wichtigkeit. Eine bunte Mischung ganz unterschiedlicher Menschen ist eine gute Voraussetzung für ein gelungenes Event.

Steht die Gästezahl fest, überlege ich mir als nächstes die Dekoration, die Sitzordnung und das Menü. Auch wenn das Essen inzwischen eine große Bedeutung bekommen hat, ist es für mich die schönste Nebensache einer Einladung. Natürlich muss es allen schmecken, aber das gemütliche Zusammensitzen mit Freunden in einem kreativen Ambiente und ein gutes Gespräch sind für mich wichtiger als eine auf Spitzengastronomie getrimmte Küche.

People are always asking me about the right time to send an invitation. There is, in fact, a quite simple rule: The more important the occasion, the sooner you should send out the invitations. This could be a couple of months in advance for a wedding, when friends from overseas are invited, or a days' notice for an informal text message invitation to a simple lunch date.

Needless to say, the number of guests I choose to invite depends on the available space. I prefer to invite fewer, but more interesting people. A potpourri of very different people is a prerequisite for a successful event.

When the number of guests is decided, I can start to think about the decoration, the seating arrangements and the menu. Although great importance is attached to the food, a cozy get-together with friends in a creative ambience with good conversation, is much more important to me than prim 5-star catering.

Geht es Ihnen nicht auch so – Jahre später erinnere ich mich, wenn ich an ein spezielles Event zurückdenke, vor allem an die Menschen, mit denen ich gesprochen habe. Versuchen Sie also nicht, einem Sternekoch Konkurrenz zu machen, sondern servieren Sie Gerichte, die Sie problemlos vorbereiten können und deren komplizierte Zubereitung Sie nicht an die Küche fesselt. Oder Sie beauftragen einfach einen guten Caterer.

Bei der Dekoration lasse ich mich von den Jahreszeiten inspirieren. Ich schaue im Garten und im Wald, was die Natur gerade anbietet, und versuche, Blüten, Blumen und Beeren mit Moos und frischen Blättern und Zweigen zu kombinieren. Ganz wichtig ist die passende Beleuchtung. Ich liebe Kerzenlicht, es ist nicht zu hell und macht ein wenig jünger. Deshalb dekoriere ich auch eine Lunchtafel mit kleinen Windlichtern oder witzigen Themenkerzen.

Lassen Sie Ihrer Fantasie freien Lauf und holen Sie sich in meinem Buch Anregungen für ungewöhnliche Tischdekorationen, die wenig kosten, aber dennoch viel Freude machen und eine besondere Atmosphäre zaubern. Erlaubt ist alles, was Ihnen gefällt. Vertrauen Sie auf Ihr Gefühl – denn nur die Events, von denen Sie selbst überzeugt sind, genießen auch Ihre Gäste.

I don't know if it is the same with you, but whenever I think back to special occasions from years ago I always remember the people I spoke to. Don't try to put the award-winning chefs out of a job, just serve food you can prepare easily and that doesn't keep you tied-up in the kitchen. Or you could simply use a good caterer.

I let the seasons inspire my table decorations. I go into the garden or the woods and see what nature has to offer. Then I combine the petals, flowers and berries with moss, fresh leaves and twigs. The right sort of lighting is important. I love candlelight, it's not so harsh and makes you look younger. I even decorate the table for a lunch with small windlights or amusingly themed candles.

Let your fantasy run free and delve into my book for suggestions for the most eclectic, inexpensive table decorations, which will bring pleasure and create a magical atmosphere. And remember, if you like it, it's allowed. Trust your instincts because the only events that your guests will enjoy are the ones that you are really happy with.

Lunch

Einladungen zum Lunch gestalte ich normalerweise kulinarisch und dekorativ nicht so aufwändig wie ein Event am Abend. Viele Gäste haben nicht den ganzen Nachmittag Zeit, sondern freuen sich einfach auf ein oder zwei gemütliche Stunden bei einem zwanglosen Essen und einem Glas Wein.

Bei den Tischdekorationen kann man mittags herrlich in bunten Farben schwelgen. Vor allem an grauen regnerischen Tagen wirkt ein mit fröhlichen Farben gedeckter Tisch ausgesprochen aufheiternd. Bunte Teller und witziges Bistro-Besteck geben der Dekoration etwas Leichtes, Ungezwungenes.

Auch das Essen sollte nicht all zu schwer sein, also serviere ich Hühnchen anstelle von Gans und einen pochierten Fisch statt eines gebackenen Karpfens. Ich bevorzuge mittags unkomplizierte Gerichte wie Pasta oder Risotto, genieße aber auch einmal die nicht nur bei meinen Kindern so beliebten Wiener Schnitzel. Davor gibt es einen großen Salat und zum Dessert selbstgebackenen Kuchen oder einfach frisches Obst.

Wer nach neuen, ausgefallenen Ideen für einen gelungenen Lunch sucht, der findet wunderbare Anregungen bei den trendigen Rezepten, die von der Kofler & Kompanie AG für dieses Buch zusammengestellt worden sind.

When I invite people for lunch, the cuisine and decorations are not as lavish as they are for an evening meal. Many of the guests do not have the whole afternoon open and are happy to enjoy a relaxed hour or two with food and wine.

You can really go over the top with brightly colored table decorations at midday, especially on gray, rainy afternoons when a cheerfully decorated table can perk everyone up. Colorful dinnerware and amusing flatware help create a light, informal atmosphere.

The food should also be light. I tend to serve chicken instead of goose and poached fish rather than baked carp. Dishes such as pasta or risotto are simple and ideal for lunch, as is my children's favorite, Viennese Schnitzel. A crisp salad makes an ideal starter, with homemade cake or simply fresh fruit for dessert.

If you are looking for new and unusual ideas for a successful lunch, you will find some wonderful suggestions for trendy recipes collected within this book, all of which were created by Kofler & Kompanie.

Cool Colors

Diese Tischdekoration garantiert gute Laune. Alles ist herrlich bunt und ansteckend fröhlich: Tischdecke, Servietten, Geschirr, Besteck und die bunten Steckschwämme, die mit den Gerberablüten um die Wette leuchten. Bei den Farbkompositionen sind Ihrer Fantasie keine Grenzen gesetzt. Je nach Laune mischt man alle möglichen Farben oder konzentriert sich auf zwei, drei Grundfarben. Die Steckschwämme können Sie im Dekorationsfachhandel kaufen und nach Herzenslust in Würfel, Rechtecke oder andere Formen zurecht schneiden. Ich baue aus den Würfeln gerne einen kleinen Blumenhügel in der Mitte des Tischs, achte dabei allerdings darauf, dass mein Arrangement nicht zu hoch wird, damit sich die Gäste über die Blumen hinweg noch in die Augen schauen können.

This table decoration guarantees a good mood. Everything is wonderfully colorful and infectiously uplifting: tablecloth, napkins, dinnerware, flatware, and the colored floral foam pinpricked with gerber daisies trying to outflower each other. Let your fantasy run wild when choosing color compositions, and if the mood strikes you, mix all manner of colors together or concentrate on two or three primary colors. The floral foam can be found in specialist decoration stores and shaped into any form that strikes your fancy, i.e., cubes, squares etc. I often build a little knoll in the middle of the table out of foam cubes, while taking care that my guests can still make eye contact over the finished flower arrangement.

Gerbera sind ideale Dekorationselemente, weil die Blüten flach und breit gefächert sind. Es gibt sie in vielen leuchtenden Farben. Einfach den Stiel kürzen und die Blüten in den Steckschwamm drücken.

Gerber daisies are ideal decorative elements because of their flat flower buds and fanned-out petals. They are also available in many bright colors. Simply shorten the stems and poke the flowers into the foam.

Nachdem bei dieser Tischdekoration die Farben Orange und Rot sehr dominant sind, habe ich als Kontrast leuchtend blaue Papierservietten gewählt. Diese Kombination ist einfach frisch und bunt.

For this table decoration I used a very dominant mixture of orange and red, then as a contrast chose vivid blue paper napkins. A simple, yet fresh and colorful combination.

Zu der fröhlich bunten Tischdekoration empfiehlt die Kofler & Kompanie AG eine zarte Perlhuhnbrust mit einer raffinierten Spinatfüllung auf einem lauwarmen Muskatkürbisgelee. Ich reiche als Dessert dazu ein erfrischendes Sorbet.

As an ideal accompaniment to the colorful table decorations, Kofler & Kompanie suggests tender guinea fowl breast with an ingenious spinach filling served on a bed of butternut squash aspic. To finish off I like to serve a refreshing sorbet as dessert.

LAUWARMES MUSKATKÜRBISGELEE

Zutaten für 4 Personen: 1 Muskatkürbis · 1 weiße Zwiebel, fein gewürfelt · 1 EL Olivenöl · 1 l Gemüsebrühe · Salz · 100 g süße Sahne · 6 g Textur Kappa Gelification

Das Kürbisfruchtfleisch grob würfeln. Mit der Zwiebel im Olivenöl andünsten, die Gemüsebrühe angießen, leicht salzen. Kürbis weich kochen. Dann abgießen, abtropfen lassen und im Mixer pürieren.

Kürbispüree durch ein Sieb in einen Topf passieren. Mit der Sahne und dem Kappapulver einmal aufkochen, bis es andickt. Auf ein mit Klarsichtfolie ausgelegtes Blech gießen und erkalten lassen. Vor dem Servieren in die gewünschte Form schneiden und im Backofen bei 60 Grad erwärmen.

SPINATGEFÜLLTE PERLHUHNBRUST

Zutaten für 4 Personen: 1 Schalotte und 1 Knoblauchzehe, fein gewürfelt · 2 EL Olivenöl · 300 g Blattspinat · Salz und Pfeffer · 200 g süße Sahne · 1 Eigelb · 2 cl Cognac · Cayennepfeffer · Muskatnuss · 4 Perlhuhnbrüste · 1 Bund Thymian

Die Schalotte und den Knoblauch in einer tiefen Pfanne in wenig Olivenöl anschwitzen. Den Spinat waschen und tropfnass dazugeben. Mit Salz und Pfeffer würzen und so lange in der Pfanne schwenken, bis er zusammengefallen ist. Dann im Mixer mit Sahne, Eigelb und Cognac pürieren, mit Salz, Cayennepfeffer und Muskatnuss abschmecken. Die Farce in einen Spritzbeutel füllen.

Den Backofen auf 160 Grad vorheizen. In die Perlhuhnbrüste mit einem Kochlöffelstiel eine Öffnung drücken und mit der Farce füllen. Das Fleisch salzen, pfeffern und im restlichen Olivenöl in einer ofenfesten Pfanne zunächst auf der Hautseite anbraten. Perlhuhnbrüste wenden, den Thymian einlegen. Im heißen Ofen 15 Minuten fertiggaren. Perlhuhnbrüste auf dem Kürbisgelee anrichten und nach Belieben ausgarnieren.

LUKE-WARM BUTTERNUT SQUASH ASPIC

Ingredients for 4 people: *1 butternut squash · 1 white onion, finely diced · 1 tbsp. olive oil · 4 cups vegetable stock · salt · 3 1/2 fl. oz. single cream · 2 tsp. Textur Kappa Gelification (gelling agent)*

Chop the squash flesh into large cubes. Sauté together with the onions in olive oil, add the vegetable stock and a pinch of salt. Cook until the squash is soft. Pour off the liquid, allow to drain and then puree in a blender.

Strain the pureed butternut squash through a sieve into a pan. Add the cream and Kappa powder, heat until it thickens. Pour onto a baking sheet covered with plastic wrap and allow to cool. Cut into the required shape and warm in the oven at 140 °F before serving.

GUINEA FOWL BREAST FILLED WITH SPINACH

Ingredients for 4 people: *1 shallot and 1 clove of garlic, finely diced · 2 tbsp. olive oil · 10 oz. spinach leaves · salt and pepper · 7 fl. oz. single cream · 1 egg yolk · 1 fl. oz. cognac · cayenne pepper · nutmeg · 4 guinea fowl breasts · 1 bunch of thyme*

Sauté the shallot and garlic in a deep pan with a little olive oil. Wash the spinach and add to the pan dripping wet. Season with salt and pepper, and swirl the pan until the spinach has wilted. Pour into a blender and mix, together with the cream, egg and cognac; season to taste with salt, cayenne pepper and nutmeg. Fill a piping bag with the puree.

Pre-heat the oven to 320 °F. Make an opening in the guinea fowl breasts with the stem of a wooden spoon and fill with the puree. Sprinkle with salt and pepper and fry on the skin side in the rest of the olive oil. Turn the guinea fowl, add the thyme and place in the oven for 15 minutes until done. Arrange the finished guinea fowl breasts on the butternut squash aspic and garnish as required.

What-a-Melon

Wenn die ersten Kastanien blühen, hole ich mir den Frühsommer ins Haus. Eine ideale "Vase" für die zarten Kastanienblüten sind aufgeschnittene Wassermelonen, die quasi als Steckschwamm dienen und die Blüten lange frisch halten. Damit das Tischtuch nicht feucht wird, lege ich ein Stück Alufolie und Kastanienblätter unter die Melonenscheiben. Auf den Blättern verteile ich noch ein paar abgezupfte Blüten. Die grüne Tischdecke und die roten Servietten und Teller sorgen zusätzlich für ein bisschen Sommer-Feeling. Natürlich kann man dicke Wassermelonenscheiben auch als Steckschale für andere Blumen verwenden, zum Beispiel für kleine Röschen.

When the first chestnut trees begin to blossom, I know it's time to bring the early spring into the house. A thickly sliced watermelon is the perfect "vase" for the delicate chestnut blossoms. The slices act as natural floral foam and help the blossoms to stay fresh. Cover a piece of aluminum foil with chestnut leaves and place it under the slices of melon to keep the tablecloth dry. Scatter some blossom buds on the leaves. The green tablecloth along with the red napkins and plates remind us of the coming summer. The novel use of the watermelon works just as well with other flowers, for example small roses.

Die Melonenteller und das rote Bistro-Besteck ergänzen meine Tisch-dekoration "What-a-Melon" geradezu ideal.

The melon dinnerware and red flatware make my "What-a-Melon" table decoration complete.

Frische, hausgemachte Pasta wird von allen Gästen sehr geschätzt. Mit gebratenen Riesengarnelen und asiatischem Pak Choi sind sie ein wahrer Gaumenschmaus. Vor dem Pastagang reiche ich gerne hauchdünn geschnittenen Parmaschinken mit Honigfeigen und Ricottaspäne.

Fresh, homemade pasta is a favorite of my guests. It is an absolute culinary feast when served with shrimps and Chinese Pak Choi. I like to serve thinly sliced Parma ham and honeyed figs filled with ricotta cheese as a starter to the pasta.

HAUSGEMACHTE BANDNUDELN

Zutaten für 4 Personen: 10 Eigelb · 1 EL Olivenöl · 100 g Semolina-Mehl · 400 g Mehl Typ 00 · Salz

Das Eigelb, das Olivenöl und das Mehl zu einem glatten geschmeidigen Nudelteig verkneten. Teig zu einer Kugel formen, in Frischhaltefolie einwickeln und bei Zimmertemperatur 1 Stunde ruhen lassen.

Den Teig in Portionen teilen und mit der Nudelmaschine zu Bahnen ausrollen. Teigbahnen mit dem entsprechenden Vorsatz in die gewünschte Breite schneiden. Nudeln mit einer Gabel zu lockeren Nestern aufrollen und auf einem bemehlten Brett etwas antrocknen lassen. Die Nudeln in kochendem Salzwasser bissfest garen, dann abgießen. Einen Teil des Kochwassers auffangen.

TAGLIATELLE MIT GARNELEN UND PAK CHOI

Zutaten für 4 Personen: 2 frische rote Chilischoten · 2 Knoblauchzehen, in Scheiben geschnitten · 2 EL Olivenöl · Salz · 12 rohe, geschälte Riesengarnelen · Pfeffer · 100 ml Cognac · 12 Mini Pak Choi, geviertelt · 100 g Butter · Basilikumblätter und Parmesanhippen zum Garnieren

Die Chilischoten mit dem Knoblauch im Olivenöl anschwitzen. Die Riesengarnelen zufügen, anbraten und mit Salz und Pfeffer würzen. Den Cognac angießen und die Garnelen flambieren. Anschließend den Pak Choi und 1/3 der Butter dazugeben. Sobald die Butter leicht goldbraun ist, 300 ml des kochenden Nudelwassers zufügen.

Die restliche Butter in Stücke schneiden und in die Sauce rühren. Etwas einkochen lassen, dann die Nudeln unterheben. Portionsweise anrichten und mit Basilikumblättern und Parmesanhippen garnieren.

HOMEMADE TAGLIATELLE

Ingredients for 4 people: 10 egg yolks · 1 tbsp. olive oil · 3 1/2 oz. semolina-flour · 14 oz. pasta flour type 00 · salt

Knead the egg yolks, olive oil and flour into a smooth pasta dough. Form into a ball, cover with plastic wrap and allow to stand for 1 hour at room temperature.

Divide the dough into portions and press into flat sheets using a pasta maker. Cut the sheets into strips of the required width. Use a fork to roll the strips into loose nests and allow to dry out a little on a floured surface. Cook the pasta in boiling salted water until al dente. Then drain, saving some of the pasta water.

TAGLIATELLE WITH SHRIMP AND PAK CHOI

Ingredients for 4 people: 2 fresh chilis · 2 garlic cloves, sliced · 2 tbsp. olive oil · salt · 12 raw, peeled shrimps · pepper · 3 1/2 fl. oz. cognac · 12 mini Pak Choi, quartered · 3 1/2 oz. butter · basil leaves and Parmesan flakes to garnish

Sauté the chilis and garlic in olive oil, add the shrimps and season with salt and pepper. Pour in the cognac and flambé the shrimps. Then add the Pak Choi and 1/3 of the butter. When the butter has lightly browned add 10 fl. oz. of the boiling pasta water.

Chop the remaining butter and stir into the sauce. Allow to reduce a little, then fold in the pasta. Arrange into portions and garnish with basil leaves and Parmesan flakes.

Herbal Paradise

Aromatische Kräuter sind nicht nur wohlriechend und dekorativ, sondern auch wohlschmeckend. Aus einem großen Eichblattsalat entferne ich das Herz und lege den Salatkopf auf eine große Platte. In die Mitte setze ich frische Kräutersorten, die man in kleinen Töpfchen kaufen kann. Während des Essens kann man sich Blättchen abzupfen und die Speisen damit würzen. Am schönsten ist es natürlich, wenn die Dekorations-Kräuter auch in den servierten Gerichten vorkommen. Sowohl den Salat als auch die Kräuter verwenden wir später in der Küche. Weggeworfen wird bei mir nichts.

Aromatic herbs are not just decorative and fragrant, they are also deliciously tasty. I take the middle out of a red oak-leaf lettuce and place the lettuce head on a large platter. Then I put fresh herbs, the sorts that you can buy in small pots, in the middle. During the meal, guests can pick the leaves and use them to season their food. It is always nice to have the same herbs in the decoration and in the food served. Later the lettuce and herbs are used in the kitchen. I don't like throwing things away.

Eine hübsche Ergänzung zur Tischdekoration sind die Kohlkopfkerzen, die auch bei Tag ein stimmungsvolles Licht geben.

Small cabbage-head candles are cute additions to the table, giving the decorations an atmospheric light.

Vor allem bei Silberbesteck kann man ganz unkonventionell auch verschiedene Modelle mischen.

Silverware can be mixed and matched; ignore convention and use dissimilar sets.

Das Carpaccio wurde von Guiseppe Cipriani in Venedig kreiert. Das Original besteht aus hauchdünn geschnittenem Rinderfilet, über das ein Mayonnaisegitter gelegt wird. Inzwischen ersetzt man das Rinderfilet häufig durch Fisch oder Gemüse. Dieses Rote Bete Carpaccio mag ich besonders gern.

Carpaccio was first created by Guiseppe Cipriani in Venice. Originally it was made from wafer-thin slices of beef fillet laid on a mayonnaise lattice. Nowadays the beef is often replaced with fish or vegetables. My favorite is beetroot Carpaccio.

ZITRONENMAYONNAISE

Zutaten für 8 Personen: 1 Ei · 1 Eigelb · Saft von 2 Zitronen · 2 EL saure Sahne · 300 ml Pflanzenöl · 100 ml Olivenöl · Salz · Pfeffer

Das Ei und das Eigelb mit dem Zitronensaft und dem Sauerrahm in ein hohes Gefäß geben. Die beiden Öle dazugießen.

Den Stabmixer in das Gefäß tauchen und langsam in kreisenden Bewegungen hochziehen, bis eine dickflüssige homogene Mayonnaise entstanden ist. Mit Salz und Pfeffer abschmecken.

LEMON MAYONNAISE

Ingredients for 8 people: *1 egg · 1 egg yolk · the juice of 2 lemons · 2 tbsp. sour cream · 10 fl. oz. vegetable oil · 3 1/2 fl. oz. olive oil · salt · pepper*

Put the egg, egg yolk, lemon juice and sour cream into a high-sided container, add both oils.

Immerse a hand mixer into the liquid and slowly lift up using a circular movement until the mayonnaise will evenly thicken. Season to taste with salt and pepper.

ROTE BETE CARPACCIO

Zutaten für 8 Personen: 8 gekochte Rote Beten · 6 eingelegte schwarze Nüsse · 100 g Wildkräuter (z.B. Kerbel, Rukola, Löwenzahn, rotes Basilikum, Schnittlauch)

Die Roten Beten in möglichst dünne Scheiben schneiden und 8 Teller damit auslegen. Die Zitronenmayonnaise mit einem Löffel gitterförmig darauf verteilen.

Die schwarzen Nüsse mit dem Trüffelhobel darüber hobeln und mit den Kräutern garnieren.

BEETROOT CARPACCIO

Ingredients for 8 people: *8 cooked beetroots · 6 preserved black nuts · 3 3/4 oz. wild herbs (e.g. chervil, arugula, dandelion, red basil, chives)*

Slice the beetroots finely and arrange onto 8 plates. Pour the lemon mayonnaise over the beetroot, using a spoon to make a lattice.

Slice the nuts with a truffle slicer and place on the lattice, garnish with the herbs.

Fruity Flowers

Wenig Aufwand – große Wirkung. Als ich zum ersten Mal auf die Idee kam, zwei verschiedene Glasvasen ineinander zu stellen und mit Früchten zu füllen, habe ich nach einer Möglichkeit gesucht, um die Früchte zu schützen und besser zur Geltung zu bringen. Sie sollen nicht gequetscht werden, denn nach dem Event wollen wir sie noch verwerten. Also fülle ich die Vasen mit Wasser und lege dann beispielsweise Trauben und Kirschen hinein. In die innere Vase stelle ich am liebsten Blütenzweige wie diese Apfelblüten oder langstielige Rosen. Die Früchte verdecken die Blumenstängel und geben dem Arrangement eine außergewöhnliche Note. Für mich ist das eine ideale Sommerdekoration.

Little effort – big effect. When I first had the idea of putting one glass vase inside another and filling it with fruit, the problem arose of how to protect the fruit. Ideally, the fruit should not get squashed, so we can salvage it after the event is over. Therefore I fill the vases with water and then place grapes and cherries inside. I prefer to put blossom twigs, such as these apple blossoms or long-stemmed roses, in the inner vase. The fruit hides the flower stems and gives the arrangement an extraordinary nuance. This is my ideal summer decoration.

Schöne Tischplatten muss man nicht verhüllen. Bei diesem alten Tisch verzichte ich auf Tischdecke oder Sets und lege unter die Vase in der Tischmitte nur einige frische Blätter aus dem Garten oder dem Wald.

A beautiful tabletop should not be covered up. I did away with the table cloth and mats for this old table and simply put some fresh leaves from the garden or the woods under a vase in the middle.

Früchte mit einer dickeren Schale wie Trauben und Kirschen können problemlos einige Stunden im Wasser liegen. Sind die Gäste wieder gegangen, gieße ich die Früchte ab und mache daraus einen köstlichen Fruchtsaft.

Thick-skinned fruit such as grapes or cherries can be left in water for many hours. Once the guests have left, I pour them out and make them into a delicious fruit juice.

Die Kombination von kross gebratenem Fisch mit fruchtigem Melonensalat und knusprigem Lauchstroh ist einfach köstlich. Dieses leichte Gericht ist ideal zum Lunch. Dazu passt ein gut gekühlter Weißwein oder ein Glas Prosecco.

The combination of fried crispy fish, fruity melon salad and crunchy leek straws is simply delicious. This light dish is perfect for lunch. A chilled white wine or a glass of Prosecco is the ideal accompaniment.

MELONENSALAT

Zutaten für 8 Personen: 1 Honigmelone · 1 Ogenmelone · 1/2 Wassermelone · 2 TL Zitronenöl · Salz · Zucker

Die Honig- und die Ogenmelone halbieren. Die Kerne aus den Melonen herauslösen. Mit einem Kugelausstecher aus dem Fruchtfleisch kleine Bällchen ausstechen. Melonenbällchen mit dem Zitronenöl beträufeln, mit Salz und Zucker würzen und etwas ziehen lassen.

MELON SALAD

Ingredients for 8 people: *1 honeydew melon · 1 cantaloupe · 1/2 water melon · 2 tsp. lemon juice · salt · sugar*

Cut the honeydew melon and cantaloupe in half and remove the seeds. Scoop out the flesh using a melon ball scoop. Sprinkle the balls with lemon juice, season with sugar and salt and allow to steep.

GEBRATENER SEEWOLF MIT LAUCHSTROH

Zutaten für 8 Personen: 1 Stange Lauch · Öl zum Frittieren · 8 Seewolffilets mit Haut · Salz · Pfeffer · 2 EL Olivenöl · Minzeblätter, Minzepesto und rote Chilisauce zum Garnieren

Das Weiße vom Lauch in hauchdünne Streifen schneiden. Öl in einer Fritteuse nicht zu stark erhitzen und die Lauchstreifen darin kurz frittieren. Auf Küchenpapier abtropfen lassen und leicht salzen.

Die Fischfilets halbieren und mit Salz und Pfeffer würzen. Das Olivenöl in einer großen Pfanne erhitzen und den Fisch auf der Hautseite darin anbraten. Fischfilets vorsichtig wenden und bei kleiner Hitze fertiggaren.

Den Melonensalat auf 8 Tellern anrichten. Fischfilets und das Lauchstroh darauf verteilen. Mit Minzeblättern, Pesto und Chilisauce garnieren.

FRIED WOLFFISH WITH LEEK STRAWS

Ingredients for 8 people: *1 leek · oil for deep-frying · 8 wolffish fillets with skin · salt · pepper · 2 tbsp. olive oil · mint leaves, mint pesto and red chili sauce to garnish*

Cut the white part of the leek into wafer-thin strips. Briefly fry the leek strips in the oil in a moderately heated deep-fryer. Place them on a paper towel and add a pinch of salt.

Halve the fish fillets and season with salt and pepper. Heat the olive oil in a large pan and fry the fish skin-side down. Carefully turn-over the fillets, reduce the heat and fry until done.

Arrange the melon balls on 8 plates. Place the fish and leek straws on top. Garnish with mint leaves, pesto and chili sauce.

Dinner

Einladungen zum Abendessen können ganz verschiedene Anlässe haben. Sie reichen vom spontanen Grillen im Garten bis hin zum gesetzten Dinner in Abendgarderobe.

Doch ganz egal, was ich plane, meine Tischdekoration basiert auch abends immer auf preiswerten Grundelementen: Blumen, Blätter und Zweige oder auch Obst und Gemüse kann man mit einfachen Stoffen, Bändern und Kerzen kombinieren – entweder farbenfroh gemischt oder klassisch in den Farben schwarz und weiß.

Ich mag Tischdecken, die bis auf den Boden reichen. Deshalb kaufe ich meist Deko-Stoffe, die nicht viel kosten und breiter sind als herkömmliche Tischdecken. Der Stoff ist schnell umgenäht und mit der entsprechenden Dekoration wirken die maßgefertigen Tischtücher richtig edel.

Schöne Platzteller sind ein zusätzlicher Blickfang. Es gibt sehr dekorative Platzteller aus ganz verschiedenen Materialien, Farben und Formen.

There are any number of reasons why you might invite people to dinner. They range from spur-of-the-moment barbecues in the garden to formal dinners with eveningwear.

But whatever the occasion, I always base my table decoration on inexpensive basic elements: flowers, leaves, twigs or fruit and vegetables. These are then combined with simple fabrics, ribbons and candles either in an exciting mix of colors or classic black and white.

I love tablecloths that are long enough to touch the floor. Therefore I buy decorative fabric, which is reasonably priced and wider than ordinary tablecloths. The fabric can be easily altered to suit the decorations and in the end has the appearance of a custom-made high-quality tablecloth.

Pretty serving plates also catch the eye. They are very decorative and come in many different colors, shapes and materials.

A Walk
in the Park

Ein Spaziergang durch den Park ist das Motto dieser Tischdekoration, das sich auch in den verwendeten Deko-Materialien widerspiegelt. Dafür verwandle ich den Tisch mit unterschiedlichen Moosarten in eine Miniatur-Waldlandschaft. In die Mooskissen werden belaubte Ästchen von Lärchen, Buchen oder Linden, Kiefern- und Lärchenzapfen sowie kleine Keramiktiere gesteckt. Bei genauerem Hinsehen entpuppen sich einige Tiere wie Hase und Dachs als Salz- und Pfefferstreuer. Anstelle einer Tischdecke lege ich schöne große Blätter, beispielsweise von Kastanien, unter die Teller. Zu dieser rustikalen Dekoration passen bodenständige Gerichte und ein kühles Bier.

'A walk in the park' is the motto for this table decoration, and it is reflected in the materials used as decorations. I've turned the table into a mini-forest using a variety of mosses. Twigs with leaves on them from the larch, beech or linden tree, pine or larch cones as well as ceramic animals are tucked into the moss landscape. If you look closely, you can see that the rabbits and badgers are actually salt and pepper shakers. Instead of a tablecloth, I lay big beautiful leaves, for example from the chestnut tree, under the plates. This rustic type of decoration is fabulous with down-to-earth food and a cold beer.

Junge Lärchen-, Buchen- und Eichenzweige kommen mit Moos und Farnen besonders gut zur Geltung. Die verschiedenen Grüntöne geben der Dekoration Frische und Lebendigkeit.

Young larch, beech and oak twigs come into their own alongside moss and ferns. The abundant shades of green give the decoration freshness and vitality.

Zu den kräftig grünen Blättern und der Mooslandschaft passt ein bäuerliches Keramikgeschirr mit farbigem Dekor. Die bunten Vögel sind kleine Kerzen.

The strong green colors of the leaves and the moss landscape go very well together with colorful rural ceramic dinnerware. The small brightly colored birds are candles.

Das Grün der Tischdekoration findet sich im köstlichen Dessert wieder. Eine besonders feine Kombination sind die aromatischen Erdbeeren mit einer zarten Mascarponecreme und dem süßen Basilikumpesto.

The green in the table decorations is also present in the delicious dessert: a particularly exquisite combination of fragrant strawberries with tender mascarpone cream and sweet basil pesto.

MASCARPONECREME

Zutaten für 8 Personen: 3 Blatt Gelatine · 4 Eier · 2 Eigelb · 200 g Zucker · Mark von 1/2 Vanillestange · 100 ml Grand Marnier · 250 g Mascarpone · 250 g süße Sahne

Die Gelatine in kaltem Wasser einweichen. Die Eier und das Eigelb mit dem Zucker und dem Vanillemark über dem heißen Wasserbad schaumig aufschlagen.

Den Grand Marnier erhitzen und die ausgedrückte Gelatine darin auflösen. Dann unter die Eischaumcreme rühren. Die Creme im kalten Wasserbad schlagen, bis sie abgekühlt ist. Den Mascarpone mit dem Handrührgerät untermischen.

Die Sahne steif schlagen und mit einem Schneebesen unter die Creme heben. In eine Schüssel umfüllen und einige Stunden kalt stellen.

MASCARPONE CREAM

Ingredients for 8 people: *3 sheets of gelatin · 4 eggs · 2 egg yolks · 7 oz. sugar · seeds from 1/2 vanilla bean · 3 1/2 fl. oz. Grand Marnier · 8 oz. mascarpone · 8 fl. oz. single cream*

Soften the gelatin in cold water. Whisk the eggs and the egg yolks together with the sugar and the vanilla seeds over a steam bath until frothy.

Heat the Grand Marnier and dissolve the gelatin into it. Then stir it into the frothy egg. Beat the mixture in a bowl of cold water until cool. Stir in the mascarpone with a hand mixer.

Beat the cream until it thickens and then fold into the mixture with a hand whisk. Transfer to a bowl and cool for a few hours.

SÜSSER MANDELPESTO MIT ERDBEEREN

Zutaten für 8 Personen: 2 Bund Basilikum · 200 ml Olivenöl · 1/2 TL Haco Weiß · 20 g Mandelblättchen · 50 g Zucker · 250 g Erdbeeren, in Scheiben geschnitten · Mandelhippen und Minzeblätter zum Garnieren

Die Basilikumblätter mit dem Olivenöl und dem Haco Weiß im Mixer pürieren. Die Mandelblättchen und den Zucker zufügen und zu einem cremigen Pesto aufmixen.

Den Pesto auf 8 Teller verteilen. Die Erdbeeren darauf anrichten. Von der Mascarponecreme mit einem Löffel Nocken abstechen und auf die Erdbeeren setzen. Mit Mandelhippen und Minzeblättern garnieren.

SWEET ALMOND PESTO WITH STRAWBERRY

Ingredients for 8 people: *2 bunches of basil · 7 fl. oz. olive oil · 1/2 tsp. Haco Weiß · 3/4 oz. flaked almond · 2 oz. sugar · 9 oz. strawberries cut into slices · almond flakes and mint leaves to garnish*

Puree the basil leaves, olive oil and Haco Weiß with a blender. Add the flaked almonds and sugar, blend into a creamy pesto.

Divide the pesto between the 8 plates and put the strawberries on top. Use a spoon to pare off dollops of mascarpone cream and sit them on the strawberries. Garnish with almond flakes and mint leaves.

Green Power

Immer wieder für Erstaunen sorgt die grüne Wiese auf dem Tisch: Rollrasen, auf dem echte Wiesenblumen, Gerbera und Kerzenwachs-Blumen blühen und sich kleine Stoffschmetterlinge tummeln. Den Rasen muss man rechtzeitig über ein Lagerhaus vorbestellen und am besten einen Tag vor dem Event auf dem Tisch auslegen. Ist er zu hoch, wird er einfach mit der Gartenschere gestutzt. Unter den Rasen sollte man eine bodenlange Tischdecke sowie Folie legen, damit die Tischplatte geschützt ist. An den Schnittkanten befestige ich mit Stecknadeln ein grünes Geschenkband. Das sieht hübsch aus und schützt die Kleidung der Gäste. Rechteckige Glasuntersetzer sorgen dafür, dass die Weingläser nicht umfallen oder im Rasen einsinken.

My green meadow table is always a cause of astonishment: rolled grass and real meadow flowers, gerber daisies and wax flowers bloom, and an abundance of cloth butterflies flitter and flutter about. You need to order the grass in good time and lay it on the table a day before the dinner. If the grass is too high simply cut it to size with garden shears. You should put a floor-length tablecloth and foil under the grass to protect the table. For the edges, I use pins to fix on green giftwrap ribbon. It is very pretty and protects the guests' clothing. Rectangular glass coasters stop the wine glasses from falling over or sinking into the grass.

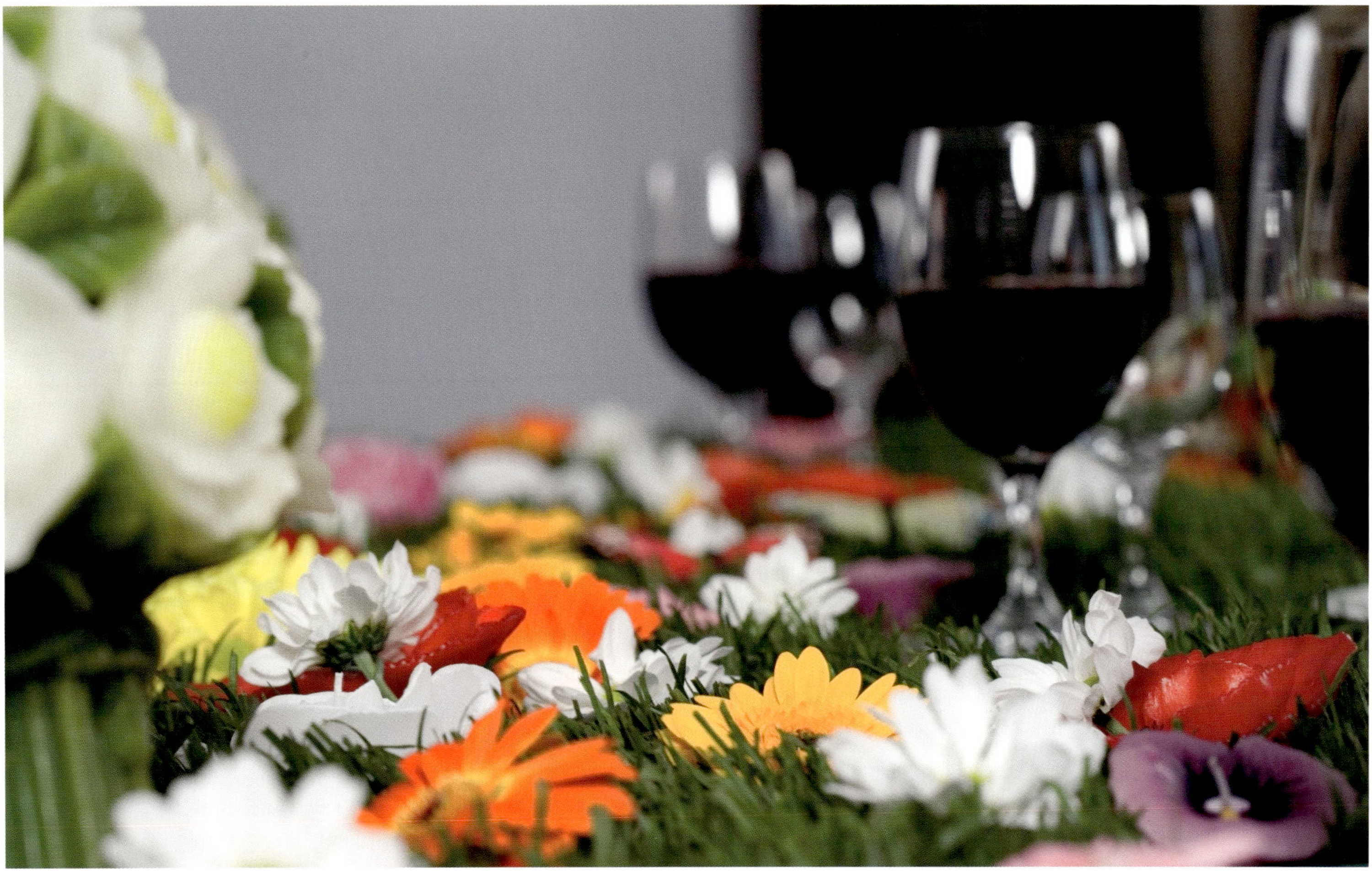

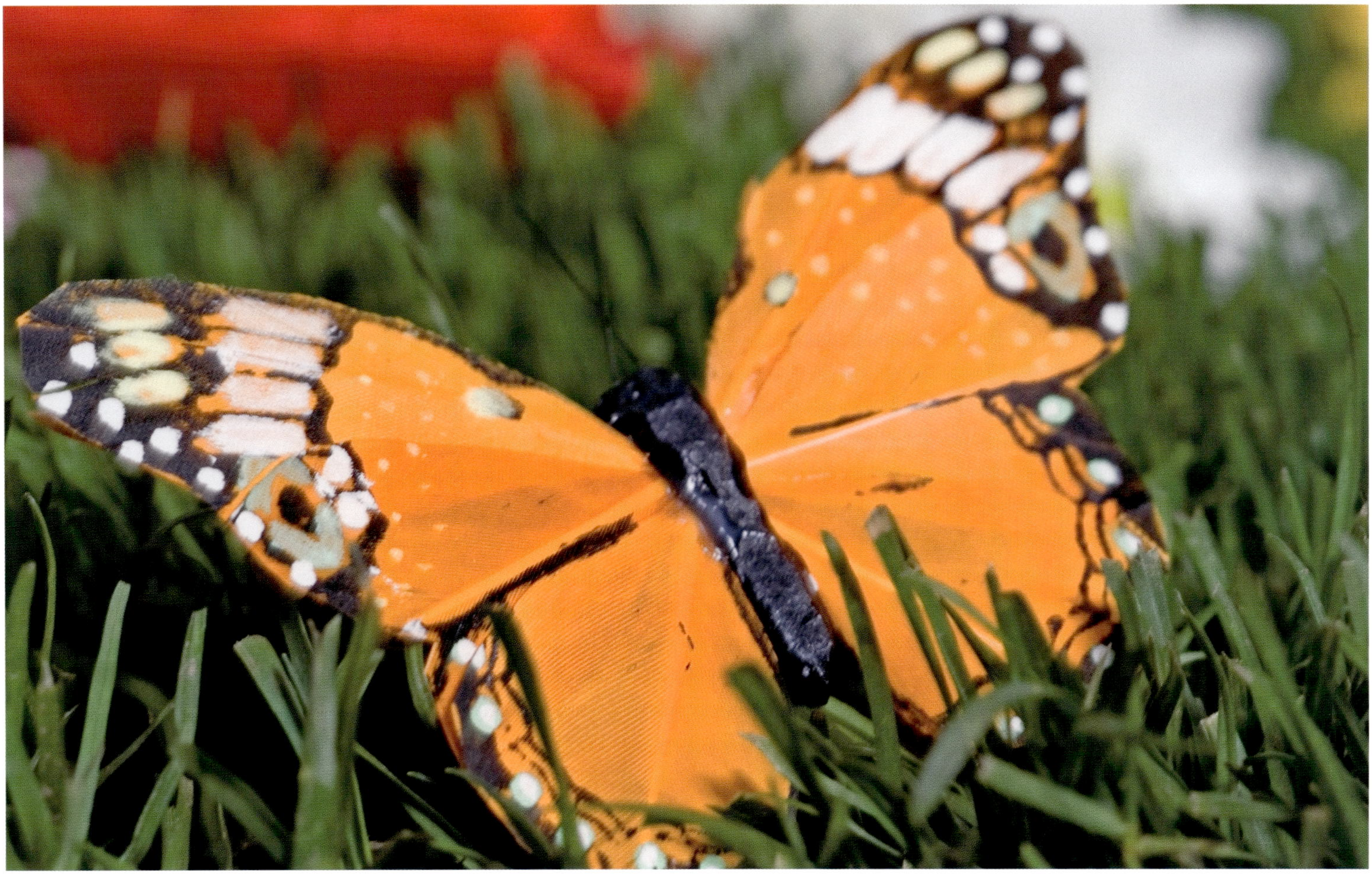

Die kleinen grünen Erbsen sind ein wahrhaft königliches Gemüse. Sie waren eine der Lieblingsspeisen des französischen Sonnenkönigs Ludwig XIV. Das feine Erbsensüppchen mit Wildlachsspießchen gehört zu meinen Favoriten.

Small green peas are a truly luxurious vegetable. They were the favorite food of the French "Sun King" Louis XIV. Green pea soup with wild salmon skewers is one of my favorite dishes.

ZWEIERLEI VON DER GRÜNEN ERBSE

Zutaten für 4 Personen: 3 Schalotten, fein gewürfelt · 3 EL Olivenöl · Zucker · 300 ml Gemüsebrühe · 200 g süße Sahne · 600 g TK-Erbsen · Cayennepfeffer · Saft von 1 Limette · 2 unbehandelte Limetten · 300 g Wildlachs · weißer Pfeffer · 4 Jakobsmuscheln · 2 Stängel Zitronengras · schwarzes Palm Island Salz · 1 TL Limettenöl · Minzeblätter zum Garnieren

Die Schalotten in 1 Esslöffel Olivenöl anschwitzen, mit Salz und Zucker würzen. Mit der Gemüsebrühe ablöschen und die Sahne zugießen. Einmal aufkochen lassen. 500 Gramm Erbsen dazugeben und den Topf vom Herd nehmen. Mit dem Stabmixer sämig aufmixen und durch ein Sieb passieren. Die Suppe mit Cayennepfeffer, Salz, Zucker und Limettensaft abschmecken. Im Kühlschrank ziehen lassen.

Die Schale von 1 Limette abreiben. Beide Limetten schälen und filetieren. Die Limettenfilets mit der abgeriebenen Limettenschale, Olivenöl und 1 Prise Zucker abschmecken.

Die restlichen Erbsen in leicht gesalzenem Wasser garen.

Den Lachs pfeffern, die Jakobsmuscheln salzen. Beides im restlichen Olivenöl glasig anbraten. Das Zitronengras längs halbieren und ein Ende anspitzen. Lachs in Würfel schneiden und auf die Zitronengrasstängel stecken.

Die Suppe in 4 Schalen verteilen, jeweils 1 Lachsspieß darauflegen, mit schwarzem Salz bestreuen und einige Tropfen Limettenöl auf die Suppe geben. Die Jakobsmuscheln portionsweise auf den Erbsen anrichten und die Limettenfilets darauf verteilen. Mit Minzeblättern garnieren.

GREEN PEAS ON THE DOUBLE

Ingredients for 4 people: *3 shallots, finely diced · 3 tbsp. olive oil · sugar · 1 1/4 cup vegetable stock · 7 fl. oz. single cream · 21 oz. frozen peas · cayenne pepper · juice of 1 lime · 2 organic limes · 11 oz. wild salmon · white pepper · 4 scallops · 2 lemon grass stems · black Palm Island salt · 1 tsp. lime oil · mint leaves for garnishing*

Sauté the shallots in 1 tbsp. of olive oil, season with sugar and salt. Add the vegetable stock and pour in the cream. Bring to a boil. Add 17 oz. of the peas and remove from the heat. Blend until thick and strain through a sieve. Season the soup to taste with sugar, salt, cayenne pepper and lime juice. Allow to marinate in the refrigerator.

Grate the rind of one lime. Peel both limes and fillet the segments. Season the lime segments with grated peel, olive oil and a pinch of sugar.

Cook the rest of the peas in lightly salted water.

Add pepper to the salmon and salt to the scallops. Fry both in the remaining olive oil until transparent. Cut the lemon grass stems in half lengthways and sharpen the ends. Cut the salmon into cubes and skewer with the lemon grass.

Divide the soup between 4 bowls, lay a salmon skewer across each one, sprinkle black salt and a few drops of lime oil on the soup. Arrange the scallops on the peas and spread the lime segments on top. Garnish with mint leaves.

Dreaming of a
White Christmas

Weihnachten ist bei uns ein fröhliches Familienfest. Die Tischdekoration darf dabei ruhig einmal etwas kitschiger ausfallen. Die Stühle bekommen Flügel und geben den Kindern das Gefühl, selbst ein Engel zu sein. Fichtenzweige mit künstlichem Schnee verbreiten Weihnachtsstimmung und der bunte Christbaumschmuck verwandelt den Tisch in einen Weihnachtsbaum. Ins richtige Licht gesetzt wird das Fest durch große "Schneekerzen". Dazu stelle ich zwei Glasvasen ineinander und fülle den Zwischenraum mit künstlichem Schnee auf. In die innere Vase kommt eine große Kerze.

Our Christmases are joyful family occasions. The table decorations are rather kitsch – the chairs grow wings, making the children fell like little angels. Spruce twigs covered with imitation snow add to the Christmassy atmosphere, and tree decorations turn the table into a Christmas tree. The festive lighting comes from "snow candles". In order to make them I put one vase inside another one and fill the space in-between with imitation snow. I then put a large candle in the inner vase.

Je nach Jahreszeit hänge ich verschiedene Dekorationen an den Leuchter über dem Esstisch. An Weihnachten nehme ich lustigen Christbaumschmuck.

I drape decorations from the lights hanging over the dinner table depending on the time of year. At Christmas I dress them with whimsical Christmas tree decorations.

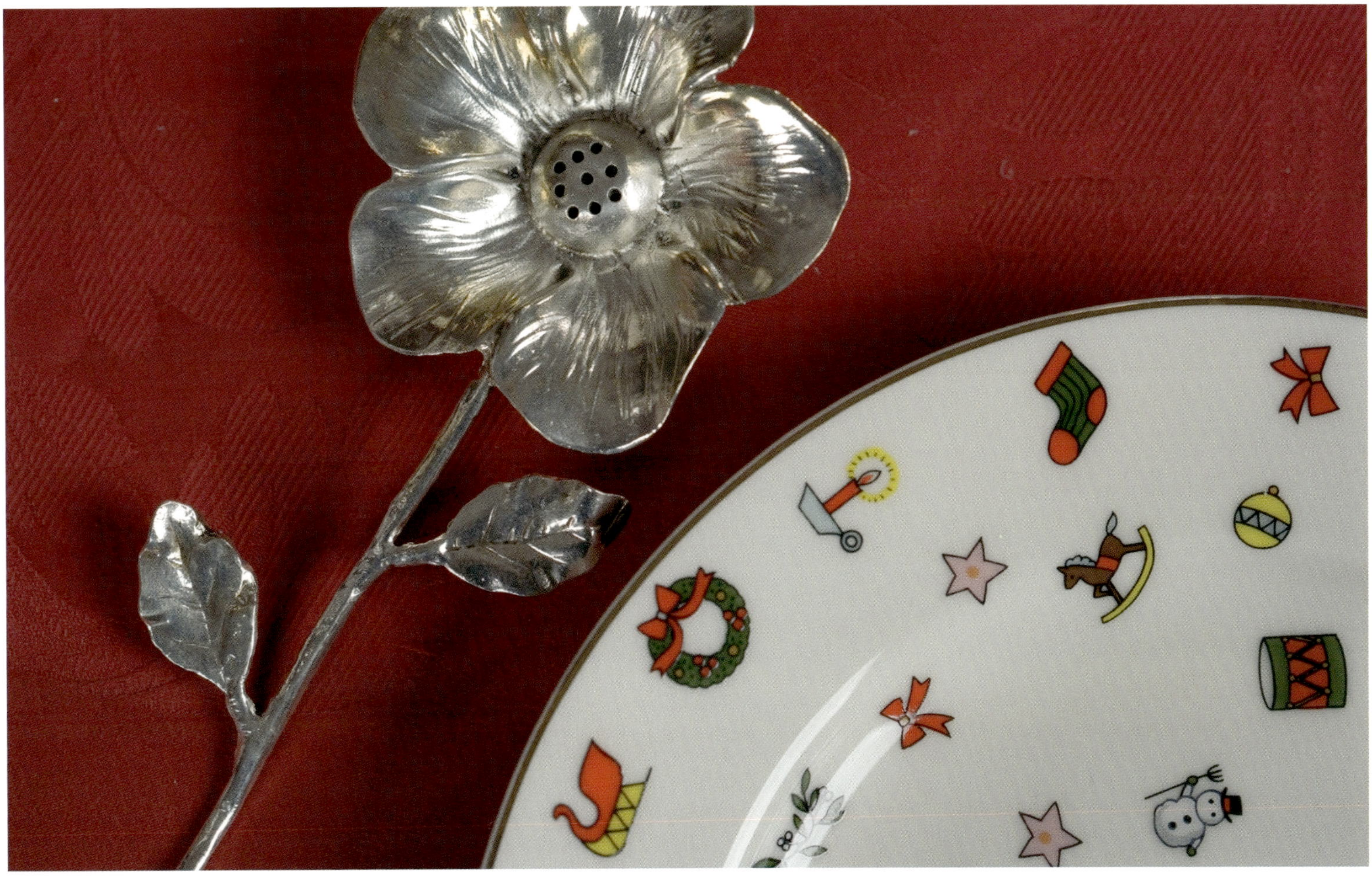

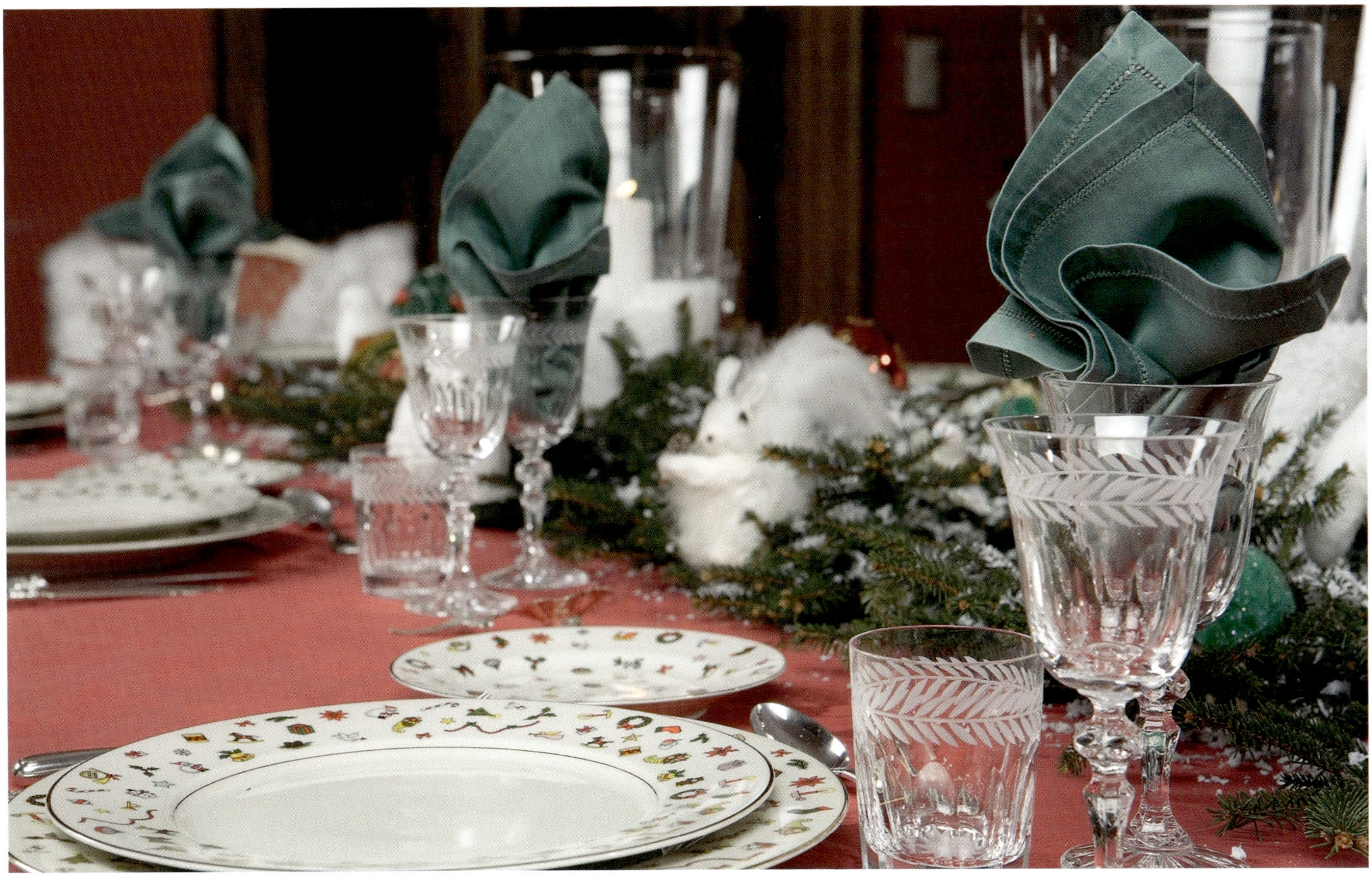

Weihnachten ist nicht nur ein Fest der Freude, sondern auch des guten Essens. Jetzt ist die Zeit der kräftigen Gewürze, deren Duft und Würze die kalte Jahreszeit versüßen. Eine kleine Sünde wert ist die Lebkuchenmousse mit dem Sahnehäubchen, das mit Tonkabohnen aromatisiert ist.

Christmas is a time for joy and good food. Now is the time to gather those Christmas spices with fragrances and flavors that best express this cold time of year. Gingerbread mousse, flavored with tonka beans and a dollop of cream, makes a delightfully naughty treat.

TONKABOHNENDUFT

Zutaten für 8 Personen: 400 g süße Sahne · 200 g Zucker · 6 Tonkabohnen

Die Sahne mit dem Zucker und den Tonkabohnen einmal aufkochen und 1 Stunde ziehen lassen. Anschließend durch ein feines Sieb passieren und in einen Sahnesiphon umfüllen. Bis zum Gebrauch kalt stellen.

LEBKUCHENMOUSSE MIT FRISCHEN WALDBEEREN

Zutaten für 8 Personen: 4 Blatt Gelatine · 5 Eier · 250 g Zucker · 1 EL Lebkuchengewürz · 2 EL brauner Rum · 250 g weiße Kuvertüre · 250 g süße Sahne · 500 g gemischte Waldbeeren (Brombeeren, Himbeeren, Blaubeeren) · Honighippen und Minzeblätter zum Garnieren

Die Gelatine in kaltem Wasser einweichen. Die Eier mit 150 g Zucker und dem Lebkuchengewürz so lange in der Küchenmaschine aufschlagen, bis eine feste Masse entsteht.

Den Rum erwärmen und die tropfnasse Gelatine darin auflösen. Die Kuvertüre über dem heißen Wasserbad schmelzen. Beides unter die Ei-Zucker-Masse rühren und im kalten Wasserbad abkühlen lassen.

Die Sahne steif schlagen und unter die Masse heben. In eine Schüssel umfüllen und 2 Stunden kalt stellen.

Den restlichen Zucker mit 100 ml Wasser aufkochen und die Hälfte der Beeren zufügen. Zum Kochen bringen, anschließend mit dem Stabmixer pürieren und durch ein Sieb passieren.

Mit einem Esslöffel von der Lebkuchenmousse Nocken abstechen. Portionsweise mit den restlichen Beeren, der Beerensauce und dem Tonkabohnenduft anrichten, mit Honighippen und Minzeblättern garnieren.

TONKA BEAN CREAM

Ingredients for 8 people: 14 fl. oz. single cream · 7 oz. sugar · 6 tonka beans

Bring the beans, cream and sugar to a boil; remove from heat and allow to stand for 1 hour. Filter through a fine sieve and pour into a piping bag. Chill before use.

GINGERBREAD MOUSSE WITH FRESH FRUITS OF THE FOREST

Ingredients for 8 people: 4 gelatin sheets · 5 eggs · 8 oz. sugar · 1 tbsp. gingerbread spice · 2 tbsp. brown rum · 8 oz. white couverture chocolate · 8 fl. oz. single cream · 16 oz. mixed forest fruits (raspberry, blueberry, blackberry) · honey flakes and mint leaves to garnish

Soften the gelatin in cold water. Mix the eggs, 5 oz. sugar and the gingerbread spice in a kitchen blender until they thicken.

Warm the rum and dissolve the gelatin into it. Melt the chocolate in a steam bath. Mix both into the egg/sugar mixture and cool in a bowl of cold water.

Whisk the cream and fold into the mixture. Transfer to a bowl and chill for 2 hours.

Heat the rest of the sugar together with 3 1/2 fl. oz. water and add half of the berries. Bring to a boil. Make into a puree and sieve.

Arrange a dollop of gingerbread mousse together with some berries and the berry sauce on a plate, add the tonka-bean cream and garnish with honey flakes and mint leaves.

Black and White

Schwarz und weiß – diese klassische Farbkomposition ist einfach elegant. Dennoch muss die Dekoration deshalb weder steif noch langweilig sein. Grundlage ist dieses Mal eine schwarze Tischdecke aus Dekostoff. Die Spitzensets sind aus einem Restposten preiswerter Meterware ausgeschnitten, die Federn bekommt man für wenig Geld im Deko-Fachhandel. Zwischen die Federn in der Tischmitte stelle ich Glaswindlichter mit Teelichtern. Die dekorative Vase habe ich günstig in einem Einrichtungsgeschäft erstanden und selbst die frischen weißen Nelken erfordern keine großen finanziellen Investitionen. Dennoch wirkt die Dekoration durch die konsequente Beschränkung auf zwei Farben ausgesprochen edel.

Black and white: the most classic, yet simple color combination. Nevertheless, such decorations do not have to be formal or boring. The basis for this idea is a black tablecloth made from furnishing fabric. The place settings are made from inexpensive fabric cut-offs and the feathers are available at arts & crafts stores. In the middle of the table among the feathers, I've placed windlights with tealight candles inside. I picked up the vases at a low cost from a furniture store and filled them with fresh white carnations. Nevertheless the decoration still comes across as elegant and refined because it is limited to two colors.

Auch Papierservietten können festlich und elegant wirken. Sie müssen nur in Farbe und Muster zur übrigen Dekoration passen.

Paper napkins can also be festive and elegant. Just be sure that they match the rest of the decorations.

Zur eleganten Schwarz-Weiß-Dekoration passen Küchenklassiker wie das feine Medaillon vom Rind. Eine besondere Note bekommt das Gericht durch das knusprige Zitronenpfeffer-Segel und die raffinierte Kombination von Spargel, Tomate und Oliven.

Kitchen classics such as beef medallions are ideally suited to black and white decorations. This dish can be enhanced with a lemon pepper sail and the tasty combination of asparagus, tomatoes and olives.

ZITRONENPFEFFER-SEGEL

Zutaten für 4 Personen: 2 Blätter Frühlingsrollenteig (Fertigprodukt) · 1 Eigelb · Zitronenpfeffer

Den Backofen auf 180 Grad vorheizen. Den Frühlingsrollenteig zu 4 Segeln zurechtschneiden. Auf ein mit Backpapier ausgelegtes Blech geben, mit dem Eigelb bestreichen und mit Zitronenpfeffer bestreuen. Im heißen Ofen ca. 7 Minuten goldbraun backen.

LEMON PEPPER SAILS

Ingredients for 4 people: 2 sheets spring roll pastry · 1 egg yolk · lemon pepper

Pre-heat the oven to 360 ° F. Cut the spring roll pastry into 4 sails. Place on a baking sheet covered with parchment paper, brush with the egg yolk and sprinkle with the lemon pepper. Heat in the oven for around 7 minutes until golden brown.

MEDAILLON VOM BLACK ANGUS RIND

Zutaten für 4 Personen: 4 Rindermedaillons vom Black Angus Rind à 180 g · Salz und Pfeffer · 1 EL Olivenöl · 12 Stangen Spargel · Zucker · 4 Schalotten, in Scheiben geschnitten · 3 Knoblauchzehen, in Scheiben geschnitten · 3 TL Butter · 50 ml Portwein · 50 ml Rotwein · einige Stängel Thymian · 100 g schwarze Oliven, entsteint · 4 Kirschtomaten

Den Backofen auf 100 Grad vorheizen. Das Fleisch mit Salz und Pfeffer würzen und in einer Pfanne im heißen Olivenöl von beiden Seiten kurz anbraten. Die Filets in eine feuerfeste Form setzen und im heißen Ofen 1 Stunde gar ziehen lassen, dabei alle 15 Minuten wenden.

Den geschälten Spargel in kochendem Salzwasser mit 1 Prise Zucker bissfest garen.

Fleisch aus dem Ofen nehmen. Den ausgetretenen Fleischsaft abgießen und beiseite stellen, das Fleisch warm halten. Die Schalotten und den Knoblauch in der Pfanne mit 2 Teelöffeln Butter goldbraun braten. Mit dem Portwein ablöschen. Wenn der Portwein fast verdampft ist, den Rotwein und den Thymian zufügen. Den Fleischsaft unterrühren und etwas einkochen. Die Sauce durch ein feines Sieb in einen kleinen Topf umgießen, mit der restlichen Butter binden und mit Salz und Pfeffer abschmecken. Die Oliven in der Sauce erwärmen.

Filets auf dem Spargel mit der Sauce anrichten, mit Tomaten und Zitronenpfeffer-Segel garnieren.

BLACK ANGUS BEEF MEDALLIONS

Ingredients for 4 people: 4 black angus beef medallions each 6 oz. · salt and pepper · 1 tbsp. olive oil · 12 asparagus spears · sugar · 4 shallots, cut into slices · 3 cloves garlic, cut into slices · 3 tsp. butter · 2 fl. oz. port · 2 fl. oz. red wine · thyme · 3 1/2 oz. black olives, without the stones · 4 cherry tomatoes

Pre-heat the oven to 210 ° F. Season the meat with salt and pepper and briefly fry on each side in a pan of hot olive oil. Transfer to an ovenproof dish and cook in the oven for an hour, turning every 15 minutes.

Peel the asparagus and cook in salted water with a pinch of sugar until al dente.

Remove the beef from the oven and pour off the juices, retaining them for later. Keep the meat warm. Fry the shallots and garlic in 2 tsp. butter until golden brown, add the port. When the port has almost evaporated add the red wine and the thyme. Stir in the meat juices and briefly bring to a boil. Pass the sauce through a sieve and transfer to a small pan. Mix in the rest of the butter and season to taste with salt and pepper. Warm the olives in the sauce.

Arrange the beef filets on the asparagus and the sauce. Garnish with tomatoes and the lemon pepper sails.

Red Carpet

Diese Tischdekoration eignet sich besonders gut für eine größere Anzahl von Gästen, da sie etwas aufwändiger ist. Mittelpunkt der festlichen Tafel ist ein dichtes Arrangement aus Wildrosenblättern auf einer roten Tischdecke. In die Blätter, die wie eine niedrige Hecke wirken, stecke ich ganz viele frische Rosenblüten, kleine Früchte wie Babyananas, Trauben, Äpfel, Kiwis und Kumquats, dekorative Gemüse wie Paprikaschoten und bunte Obst-Kerzen. Die hohen Kerzenleuchter werden mit rotem Geschenkband umwickelt und mit künstlichen Himbeer- und Brombeerzweigen verziert.

This table decoration is ideal when you have a large number of guests, because it is somewhat time-consuming. The focal point of this festive table is the dense arrangement of wild rose leaves on a red tablecloth. The leaves take on the form of a low hedge that I intersperse with numerous fresh rose buds, small fruits such as baby bananas, grapes, apples, kiwis and kumquats, decorative vegetables such as capsicum and colorful fruit candles. The long candlestick holder is wrapped in gift ribbon and hung with imitation raspberries and blackberries.

Rotes Geschenkbank wird mit Stecknadeln entlang der Tischplatte am Dekostoff befestigt. Dadurch wirkt selbst einfacher Stoff wie eine kostbare Tischdecke.

*Red gift ribbon is pinned to the tablecloth along the edge of the table top trans-
forming the simple fabric into an elegant table covering.*

Langusten zählen zu den delikatesten Krustentieren. Sie werden frisch angeboten, doch nicht jeder Hobbykoch bringt es fertig, die Tiere kopfüber ins kochende Wasser zu werfen. Deshalb greifen viele auf tiefgekühlte Langustenschwänze zurück.

Crawfish are a real delicacy among shellfish. You can buy them fresh, but some amateur cooks may baulk at tossing them into boiling water. Many people use deep-frozen crawfish tails instead.

PAPAYARELISH

Zutaten für 4 Personen: 250 g Zucker · 250 ml Weißweinessig · 2 frische rote Chilischoten · 1 TL Korianderkörner · 2 Papayas

Den Zucker mit dem Essig aufkochen. Die halbierten Chilischoten und die Korianderkörner dazugeben.

Die Papayas schälen, halbieren und mit einem Löffel die Kerne herausschälen. Das Fruchtfleisch in kleine Würfel schneiden und im Essig-Zucker-Sud bei kleiner Hitze bissfest garen. Vom Herd nehmen und abkühlen lassen.

PAPAYA RELISH

Ingredients for 4 people: *9 oz. sugar · 8 1/2 fl. oz. whitewine vinegar · 2 fresh chilis · 1 tbsp. coriander seeds · 2 papayas*

Heat the sugar and the vinegar, add the halved chilis and coriander seeds.

Peel the papayas, cut in half and scoop out seeds. Cut the flesh into small cubes and cook in the sugar-vinegar mixture until al dente. Remove from heat and allow to cool.

LANGUSTE MIT AVOCADO

Zutaten für 4 Personen: 2 Avocados · Saft von 1 Limette · Salz · 2 EL Olivenöl · 2 gekochte Langustenschwänze · frische Kräuter zum Garnieren

Die Avocados halbieren und vom Kern drehen. Das Fruchtfleisch im Ganzen aus der Schale lösen, in Scheiben schneiden und mit dem Limettensaft beträufeln. Avocados salzen, mit dem Olivenöl beträufeln und etwas ziehen lassen.

Die Langustenschwänze der Länge nach halbieren, das Fleisch herauslösen und aufschneiden. Mit den marinierten Avocados und dem Papayarelish anrichten und mit Kräutern garnieren.

CRAW FISH WITH AVOCADO

Ingredients for 4 people: *2 avocados · juice of 1 lime · salt · 2 tbsp. olive oil · 2 cooked crawfish tails · fresh herbs to garnish*

Halve the avocados and remove stones. Tease the fruit from the shell and cut into slices, sprinkle with lime juice. Add salt to the avocados, sprinkle with olive oil and allow to stand.

Cut the crawfish tails in half lengthways, loosen and cut out the flesh. Arrange on a plate together with the marinated avocados and papaya relish and garnish with herbs.

BBQ in Red

Im Sommer grillen wir gerne und so oft es geht. Am liebsten sitzen wir dann mit den Kindern und Freunden an einem großen Holztisch. In ausgehöhlte Paprikaschoten stelle ich kleine Teelichter. Das gibt in der Dunkelheit ein wunderschönes, warmes Licht und sieht sehr dekorativ aus. Die Tischsets kommen aus dem Baumarkt: Ich kaufe Tapetenreste und schneide sie passend zurecht. Ein Tipp: Wenn ich zu einem Dinner im Freien einlade, plane ich parallel dazu immer eine Alternative im Haus, falls uns das Wetter einen Streich spielt.

In summer I like to barbecue as often as possible. I love to sit around a large wooden table with my friends and children. When it gets dark the small tealights I put inside hollow capsicums emit a warm light and look very decorative. The place settings are from the hardware store: I buy carpet off-cuts and cut them to size. My tip: Whenever you invite people to an alfresco dinner always plan a parallel alternative indoors. Sometimes the weather can play tricks on you.

Es muss nicht immer Fleisch sein. Ganze Fische eignen sich auch wunderbar zum Grillen. Dazu passt der toskanische Brotsalat ganz hervorragend. Man kann ihn gut vorbereiten und er schmeckt dennoch herrlich frisch.

It doesn't always have to be meat. Whole fish are exquisite on the BBQ, and a Tuscany bread salad is a perfect accompaniment. You can prepare the salad in advance and it still tastes wonderfully fresh.

TOSKANISCHER BROTSALAT

Zutaten für 8 Personen: 400 g toskanisches Landbrot vom Vortag · 1 kleine Salatgurke · 500 g Tomaten · 2 rote Zwiebeln · 100 ml Olivenöl · 2–3 EL Rotweinessig · Salz und Pfeffer · 12 Basilikumblätter

Das Weißbrot in etwa 2 cm dicke Scheiben schneiden und in einer Schüssel mit kaltem Wasser knapp 10 Minuten einweichen.

Die Gurke schälen, der Länge nach halbieren und entkernen. Gurkenhälften in dünne Halbmonde schneiden. Die Tomaten waschen und ohne Stielansatz in Scheiben schneiden. Die Zwiebeln in dünne Ringe hobeln.

Die Brotscheiben gut ausdrücken und in mundgerechte Stücke schneiden. In einer beschichteten Pfanne die Hälfte des Olivenöls erhitzen und das Brot darin unter Wenden anbraten. Vom Herd nehmen und auskühlen lassen.

Das restliche Öl mit Salz, Pfeffer und dem Essig verrühren. Gurke, Tomaten, Zwiebeln und das geröstete Brot in einer Schüssel mit dem Dressing vermischen. Die Basilikumblätter hacken und über den Salat geben. Portionsweise anrichten.

GEGRILLTE FISCHE MIT ROSMARIN

Zutaten für 8 Personen: 2 frische Fische à ca. 1,2 kg, küchenfertig (z. B. Dorade, Red Snapper oder Erdbeergrouper) · Salz und Pfeffer · 8 Zweige Rosmarin · Olivenöl zum Bestreichen

Die Fische waschen, trockentupfen und innen salzen und pfeffern. In jeden Fisch 2 Zweige Rosmarin legen und die Fische mit Olivenöl bestreichen.

Auf dem Grill bei mittlerer Hitze auf jeder Seite 8–10 Minuten grillen. Wenn der Fisch fast gar ist, den restlichen Rosmarin so in die Glut legen, dass der Fisch im aufsteigenden aromatisierten Rauch liegt. Der Fisch ist fertig, wenn sich eine Rückenflosse leicht herausziehen lässt.

TUSCANY BREAD SALAD

Ingredients for 8 people: 14 oz day-old Tuscany bread · 1 small cucumber · 1 lb tomatoes · 2 red onions · 3 1/2 fl. oz. olive oil · salt and pepper · 2–3 tbsp. red wine vinegar · 12 basil leaves

Cut the bread into slices about 1 in. thick and soften them in a bowl of cold water for about 10 minutes.

Peel the cucumber, cut in half lengthways and remove seeds. Cut the cucumber halves into thin half-moons. Wash the tomatoes and slice without the inner stem. Shave the onions into thin rings.

Press the water out of the slices of bread and cut into mouth-sized pieces. Heat half the olive oil in a coated pan and fry the bread, turning it frequently. Remove from the heat and allow to cool.

Mix the rest of the oil with salt, pepper and the vinegar. Put the cucumber, tomatoes, onions and bread into a bowl and mix in the dressing. Chop the basil leaves and sprinkle over the salad. Arrange into portions.

BARBECUED FISH WITH ROSEMARY

Ingredients for 8 people: 2 fresh fish each ca. 2 1/2 lb, ready to cook (i.e. dorado, red snapper or coral cod) · salt and pepper · 8 twigs of rosemary · olive oil for brushing

Wash the fish, pat dry, sprinkle with salt and pepper inside. Put two twigs of rosemary in each fish and brush with oil.

Grill for 8–10 minutes on each side over a medium-hot barbecue. When the fish is almost done, put the rest of the rosemary into the hot coals so that the rising aromatic smoke flavors the fish. The fish is done when the back fin can be easily pulled off.

Special Events

Neben Lunch und Dinner gibt es für mich noch ganz spezielle Anlässe für eine Einladung zum Essen. Einer ist sehr persönlich: Ich koche gerne mit Freunden. Gegessen wird dann einfach in der Küche. In diesem Fall verzichte ich auf jegliche Art von Dekoration, die beim Kochen nur stören würde.

Für geschäftliche Besprechungen habe ich eine neue Art der Bewirtung entdeckt, das "Flying Dinner". Dabei wird ein mehrgängiges Menü in kleinen Häppchen an Stehtischen serviert. Man hat keinen festen Platz, sondern kann zwischen den Gängen den Tisch und damit auch die Gesprächspartner wechseln. Gerade nach längeren Meetings ist diese kommunikative, zwanglose Form des Essens sehr angenehm. Sie gibt einem die Möglichkeit, mit vielen Menschen zu sprechen und dabei dennoch ausgesuchte Köstlichkeiten zu genießen.

In addition to lunch and dinner there are some very special occasions worthy of an invitation for a meal. One occasion is very close to my heart: I love cooking with friends. We then simply eat in the kitchen. On these occasions I do away with any kind of decoration as they would only be a hindrance during the cooking.

I have discovered a new way of entertaining my guests at business conferences – the "Flying Dinner". This involves serving several courses of a menu in small portions at bar tables. The guests don't have a designated seat and can change tables and therefore conversational partners between courses. This communicative and informal way of eating is very convenient, in particular after long meetings. It offers you the chance to talk to many people and at the same time savor a selection of delectable foods.

Cool in the Kitchen

Wer Freude am Kochen hat, ist gern gesehener Gast in meiner Küche. Hier ist die Essenszubereitung das eigentliche Event. Gemeinsam kann man auch etwas zeitaufwändigere Gerichte mit viel Spaß zubereiten. Man teilt sich die Arbeit und genießt dabei ein gutes Glas Wein. Damit wir nicht stundenlang auf das Essen warten müssen, bereite ich Grundzutaten, beispielsweise Nudelteig oder einen Fond, rechtzeitig vor. Hat man dann einen Profi wie Klaus Peter Kofler als freundschaftliche Küchenhilfe, gelingen auch Ravioli im Handumdrehen.

I always enjoy having people in my kitchen who love cooking. In this case the preparation of the food is the main event. Even the most time-consuming of dishes can be prepared together with much fun. You share the work and at the same time enjoy a glass of good wine. I prepare staples such as pasta dough or stock in advance, so we don't have to wait for hours for the food to be ready. And if you have a professional such as Klaus Peter Kofler as a friendly kitchen helper, even ravioli can be prepared in the twinkling of an eye.

Schwarze Nudeln sind ein echter Hingucker – vor allem, wenn sie so verführerisch mit roten Beeren, frischen Kräutern und Spargel serviert werden. Die Zubereitung ist zwar ein wenig aufwändig, aber das Ergebnis erfreut den Gaumen und das Auge.

Black pasta is a real head-turner – especially when served in such a tempting way with red berries, fresh herbs and asparagus. The preparation may be a little laborious but the results please the taste buds as well as the eye.

SCHWARZE RAVIOLI MIT SPARGEL UND WALDBEEREN

Zutaten für 8 Personen: 13 Eigelb · 3 EL Olivenöl · 1 TL Sepiatinte · 100 g Semolina-Mehl · 400 g Mehl Typ 00 · Salz · 3 Kartoffeln · je 12 Stangen weißer und grüner Spargel · 300 g geriebener Parmesan · 2 EL fein gehackter Majoran · Pfeffer · Muskatnuss · 1 Ei · 200 g Butter· 300 g gemischte Waldbeeren · Crema di Balsamico (Balsamicoreduktion) · gemischte Kräuter zum Garnieren

10 Eigelb, 1 Esslöffel Olivenöl, die Sepiatinte und das Mehl zu einem glatten geschmeidigen Nudelteig verkneten. Den Teig zu einer Kugel formen, in Frischhaltefolie wickeln und bei Zimmertemperatur 1 Stunde ruhen lassen.

Die Kartoffeln in Salzwasser weich kochen, abgießen, schälen und noch warm durch die Kartoffelpresse drücken. Etwas auskühlen lassen.

Den Spargel putzen und schälen, die Spargelspitzen beiseite stellen. Den Rest in kleine Würfel schneiden, in 1 Esslöffel Olivenöl anbraten und salzen. Dann mit der Kartoffelmasse, den restlichen Eigelb, dem Parmesan und 1 Esslöffel Majoran vermengen, mit Salz, Pfeffer und Muskatnuss abschmecken und in einen Spritzbeutel füllen.

Den Teig halbieren und mit der Nudelmaschine zu zwei 4 mm dünnen Bahnen ausrollen. Auf eine Teigbahn in regelmäßigen Abständen etwas Füllung setzen. Das Ei mit wenig Wasser verquirlen und die entstandenen Zwischenräume damit bestreichen. Die zweite Teigbahn darüber legen und jeweils um die Füllung herum leicht andrücken. Ravioli ausstechen und antrocknen lassen. Dann in kochendem Salzwasser garen und abgießen.

Die Spargelspitzen im restlichen Olivenöl anbraten. Mit 300 ml Wasser ablöschen, den übrigen Majoran zufügen und die Butter unterziehen. Ravioli in die Sauce geben und die Beeren unterheben. Portionsweise anrichten und mit Kräutern garnieren.

BLACK RAVIOLI WITH ASPARAGUS AND WILD BERRIES

Ingredients for 8 people: *13 egg yolks · 3 tbsp. olive oil · 1 tsp. sepia ink · 3 1/2 oz. semolina flour · 14 oz. pasta flour type 00 · salt · 3 potatoes · 12 white and 12 green asparagus spears · 10 oz. grated Parmesan cheese · 2 tbsp. finely chopped marjoram · pepper · nutmeg · 1 egg · 7 oz. butter · 10 oz. mixed wild berries · Crema di Balsamico · mixed herbs for garnishing*

Mix 10 egg yolks, 1 tbsp. olive oil, the sepia ink and the flour. Knead into a pasta dough until smooth. Form the dough into a ball, wrap in plastic wrap and leave for 1 hour at room temperature.

Boil the potatoes in salted water until soft and drain. Peel and press the warm potatoes through a ricer. Allow to cool briefly.

Clean and peel the asparagus, putting the tips aside. Chop the remaining asparagus into small cubes, fry in 1 tbsp. olive oil and add salt. Then mix the asparagus cubes, potato, the remaining egg yolk, the Parmesan and 1 tbsp. marjoram, flavor with salt, pepper and nutmeg and pour the mixture into a piping bag.

Cut the dough in half and roll it out with the pasta machine into two 1/8 inch-thick sheets. Place small dollops of the filling at regular intervals onto one sheet of dough. Whisk the egg with some water and spread it over the gaps between the filling. Place the second sheet of dough on top and press down slightly around the filling. Cut out the ravioli and briefly allow to dry. Cook in boiling, salted water until al dente, then drain.

Fry the asparagus tips in the rest of the olive oil. Quench with 10 fl. oz. of water, add the spare marjoram and fold in the butter. Add the ravioli to the sauce and fold in the wild berries. Arrange into portions and garnish with herbs.

Das richtige Timing ist beim gemeinsamen Kochen doppelt wichtig, damit man sich nicht gegenseitig im Weg steht oder das Dessert vor dem Hauptgang fertig ist. Von den Profiköchen habe ich gelernt, wie wichtig das "mise en place" ist. Darunter versteht man die Planung des Arbeitsablaufs und die Vorbereitung der Zutaten. Stehen auch die Küchengeräte einsatzbereit in Griffnähe, dann gelingt selbst ein Schokoladensoufflé leicht und spielerisch.

When cooking together with other people, timing is doubly important in order to avoid standing in each other's way or having the dessert ready before the main course. I learned the importance of the "mise en place" from professional chefs. This guides the planning of the work process and the preparation of the ingredients. If the kitchen equipment is close at hand and ready to use, even a chocolate soufflé can be prepared quickly and easily.

Glitzernde Zuckerverzierungen geben jedem Dessert eine festliche Note. Dafür kocht man einen hellen Karamell, gießt ihn in einem gleichmäßigen Strahl in der gewünschten Form auf eine Silikonmatte und lässt ihn erkalten.

Shiny decorations made from sugar give any dessert a festive note. To create them you make a light caramel, then pour it in the desired form with an even stream onto a silicone mat and let it cool.

EISENKRAUT-SORBET

Zutaten für 8 Personen: 120 g getrocknetes Eisenkraut · 120 g Glucose · 110 g Zucker · 100 ml Limejuice

Das Eisenkraut in 500 ml Wasser einmal aufkochen und ca. 20 Minuten ziehen lassen. Dann durch ein feines Sieb in einen Topf umgießen. Mit Glucose, Zucker und Limejuice nochmals aufkochen. In eine Eisschale umfüllen und 4 Stunden im Tiefkühlschrank gefrieren lassen.

VERBENA SORBET

Ingredients for 8 people: *4 oz. dried verbena · 4 oz. glucose · 3 1/2 oz. sugar · 3 1/2 fl. oz. lime juice*

Bring the verbena briefly to a boil in 17 fl. oz. of water and allow to steep for about 20 minutes. Pour through a fine sieve into a pan. Add glucose, sugar and lime juice and let the mixture boil again. Transfer to a freezer-proof bowl and chill for 4 hours in the deep-freeze.

SCHOKOLADENKUCHEN

Zutaten für 8 Personen: 250 g Butter · 160 g Zucker · 5 Eier · 5 Eigelb · 200 g flüssige Zartbitter-Kuvertüre · 1 EL Rum · 160 g Mehl · 1 TL Backpulver · Butter und Zucker für die Förmchen · Puderzucker und Minzeblätter zum Garnieren

Den Backofen auf 180 Grad Umluft vorheizen. Die Butter mit dem Zucker schaumig aufschlagen. Nach und nach die Eier und das Eigelb unterrühren. Zuletzt die flüssige Kuvertüre und den Rum unter Rühren in dünnem Strahl dazugießen.

Das Mehl sieben und unter den Teig rühren. Kleine feuerfeste Weckgläser ausbuttern und mit Zucker ausstreuen. Den Teig in einen Spritzbeutel geben und in die Gläser einfüllen, dabei die Gläser nur zu 2/3 füllen, weil der Teig beim Backen aufgeht.

Kuchen im heißen Ofen 12 Minuten bei Umluft backen. Etwas auskühlen lassen, dann aus der Form lösen und auf einem Kuchengitter auskühlen lassen.

Schokoladenkuchen mit Eisenkraut-Sorbet-Nocken anrichten, mit Puderzucker bestäuben und mit Minzeblättern garnieren.

CHOCOLATE CAKE

Ingredients for 8 people: *9 oz. butter · 5 1/2 oz. sugar · 5 eggs · 5 egg yolks · 7 fl. oz. liquid dark chocolate couverture · 1 tbsp. rum · 6 oz. flour · 1 tsp. baking powder · butter and sugar for the baking tins · powdered sugar and mint leaves for garnishing*

Pre-heat a convection oven to 350 °F. Beat butter and sugar until light and fluffy. Mix in the eggs and egg yolks a little at a time. Finally stir in the liquid chocolate couverture and the rum in a thin stream.

Sieve the flour and fold into the dough. Butter some small oven-proof preserving jars and sprinkle with sugar. Put the dough into a piping bag and fill the jars 2/3 full, as the dough will rise during the baking process.

Bake the cakes in the hot convection oven for 12 minutes. Allow the cakes to cool briefly, knock them out of the jars and allow to cool on a rack.

Arrange the chocolate cakes with spoonfuls of verbena sorbet and garnish with the powdered sugar and mint leaves.

Flying Dinner

Das Flying Dinner ist eine besonders kommunikative Form der Gäste-bewirtung. Man genießt kleine kulinarische Kunstwerke in lockerer Atmosphäre an Stehtischen. Ideal ist ein Menü mit sechs bis acht Gängen, wobei die einzelnen Gerichte vom Servicepersonal an die Tische gebracht werden. So kann man sich voll und ganz auf seine Gäste konzentrieren. Um die Vorteile dieser neuen Bewirtungsform in vollen Zügen genießen zu kön-nen, sollte man einen kreativen und erfahrenen Caterer wie die Kofler & Kompanie AG mit dem Handling beauftragen.

The Flying Dinner is a particular communicative form of catering for guests. Small culinary delicacies can be enjoyed at bar tables in a relaxed atmosphere. A menu of six to eight courses is ideal. Each individual course is brought to the tables by the service personnel, leaving you free to concen-trate fully on your guests. To appreciate all the advantages of this type of gastronomy, a creative and experienced caterer, such as Kofler & Kompanie AG should be used.

Krustenbrötchen sind eine ideale Unterlage für kleine Häppchen, die man zum Aperitiv reicht. In dünne Scheiben geschnitten und knusprig geröstet kann man sie auf vielerlei Arten belegen und garnieren.

Crusty bread rolls are an ideal basis for little snacks to go with an aperitif. Cut into thin slices and roasted until crispy, they can be garnished with a multitude of toppings.

SCHNITTLAUCHBROT

Zutaten für 4 Personen: 1 Krustenbrötchen · Pflanzenöl zum Frittieren · Salz · 100 g Butter · 1 EL fein geschnittene Schnittlauchröllchen · einige Spritzer Tabasco · 5 Radieschen, in dünne Scheiben gehobelt · 5 eingelegte Jalapenoschoten, in Scheiben geschnitten · Schnittlauchröllchen zum Garnieren · grob gemahlener Pfeffer

Das Krustenbrötchen in 16 dünne Scheiben schneiden. In heißem Öl goldbraun ausbacken und auf Küchenpapier abtropfen lassen. Anschließend leicht salzen.

Die Butter schaumig schlagen und den Schnittlauch untermischen. Mit Tabasco und Salz abschmecken und in einen Spritzbeutel füllen.

Schnittlauchbutter in kleinen Tupfen in die Mitte der Brote setzen. Mit Radieschen, Jalapenos und Schnittlauch garnieren und mit Pfeffer würzen.

CHIVE BREAD

Ingredients for 4 people: *1 crusty bread roll · vegetable oil for frying · salt · 3 1/2 oz. butter · 1 tbsp. finely chopped chives · a dash of Tabasco · 5 radishes, thinly sliced · 5 preserved jalapenos, sliced · chives for garnishing · coarsely ground pepper*

Cut the crusty bread into 16 thin slices. Fry in oil until golden brown and allow to dry on a paper towel. Then add a little salt.

Beat the butter until it is light and fluffy and mix in the chives. Season to taste with Tabasco and salt. Transfer to a piping bag.

Pipe a small dollop of chive butter onto the middle of the sliced bread. Garnish with radish, jalapenos and chopped chives, season with pepper.

Der Jamon Ibérico Bellota, wie dieser exquisite Schinken auf spanisch heißt, ist eine einzigartige Delikatesse und wird von vielen Feinschmeckern als der beste Schinken der Welt bezeichnet. Er stammt vom hinteren Teil iberischer Schweine, die wegen ihrer schwarzen Hufe auch "Pata Negra" genannt werden.

Jamon Ibérico Bellota is the name of an exquisite ham from Spain. It is an inimitable delicacy and considered to be the best ham in the world by many food connoisseurs. It comes from the hind part of the Iberian pig, also known as "pata negra" because of its black hooves.

BELLOTA SCHINKEN

Zutaten für 4 Personen: 1 Glas Ysopkirschen · 3 Blatt Gelatine · 1 TL Kirschwasser · Zucker · 16 dünne Scheiben Ochsenbrot, ca. 7 mm dick · 16 Scheiben spanischer Bellota Schinken · Sisho-Kresse und Fleur de Sel zum Garnieren

Die Kirschen abgießen, dabei den Saft auffangen. Kirschen in kleine Würfel schneiden. Die Gelatine in kaltem Wasser einweichen.

Kirschsaft auf die Hälfte einkochen, dann die ausgedrückte Gelatine in der heißen Flüssigkeit auflösen. Das Kirschwasser einrühren, mit Zucker abschmecken und die Kirschen untermischen. Kalt stellen.

Die Brotscheiben in 4,5 x 2 cm große Rechtecke schneiden und in einer Gußeisenpfanne auf beiden Seiten knusprig anrösten.

Die Schinkenscheiben auf der Arbeitsfläche auslegen und mit der Kirschmasse füllen. Schinkenscheiben über der Kirschfüllung einrollen und mit einem scharfen Messer zu 4,5 cm langen Stücken aufschneiden.

Schinkenrollen auf die Brotscheiben setzen. Mit Sisho-Kresse und Fleur de Sel garnieren.

BELLOTA HAM

Ingredients for 4 people: *1 jar Ysop cherries · 3 gelatin sheets · 1 tsp. kirsch · sugar · 16 thin slices of barley bread, around 1/4 inch thick · 16 slices of Spanish Bellota ham · red cress and Fleur de Sel to garnish*

Drain the cherries, retaining the juice. Cut into small cubes. Soften the gelatin in cold water.

Heat the cherry juice and reduce by half, dissolve the gelatin into the hot liquid. Stir in the kirsch and season to taste with sugar, add the cherries, allow to cool.

Cut the slices of bread into 2 x 1 inch rectangles and roast until crispy in a cast-iron frying pan.

Lay the ham slices on a work surface and fill with the cherry mixture. Roll into tubes and cut into 2 inch long pieces with a sharp knife.

Place the rolls of ham on the bread and garnish with red cress and Fleur de Sel.

Bei diesem asiatisch angehauchten Fingerfood kommt es vor allem auf die Qualität des Thunfischs an. Da der Fisch fast roh verzehrt wird, muss er absolut frisch sein. Verlangen Sie deshalb beim Fischhändler Thunfisch in Sushi-Qualität.

The quality of the tuna is of great importance for this fingerfood with an Asian touch. It has to be absolutely fresh as the fish is eaten almost raw. You should therefore ask the fishmonger for tuna of sushi quality.

MAGURO

Zutaten für 4 Personen: 2 reife Avocados · Saft von 1 Zitrone · 3 EL Olivenöl · Fleur de Sel · 1 Ciabatta Brötchen · 300 g frischer Thunfisch am Stück · 2 EL Paradieskörner (Guineapfeffer) · frittierte Petersilienblätter zum Garnieren

Die Avocados halbieren, vom Stein drehen und das Fruchtfleisch auslösen. Im Mixer mit dem Zitronensaft und 2 Esslöffeln Olivenöl cremig aufmixen und mit Fleur de Sel abschmecken.

Das Ciabatta mit der Aufschnittmaschine in ca. 7 mm dünne Scheiben schneiden. Die Brotscheiben anschließend in 2,5 cm große Quadrate schneiden und in einer Eisenpfanne ohne Fett von beiden Seiten knusprig braten.

Den Thunfisch in ca. 3 cm breite Streifen schneiden. Die Streifen in den Paradieskörnern wenden und rundum im restlichen Olivenöl nur kurz anbraten. Der Fisch muss innen noch roh bleiben. Die Thunfischstreifen in 1 cm dünne Scheiben schneiden.

Die Brotstücke mit Avocadocreme bestreichen und die Fischscheiben darauf setzen. Leicht mit Fleur de Sel würzen und mit den frittierten Petersilienblättern garnieren.

MAGURO

Ingredients for 4 people: *2 ripe avocados · juice of 1 lemon · 3 tbsp. olive oil · Fleur de Sel · 1 Ciabatta bread · 10 oz. piece of fresh tuna · 2 tbsp. rains of Paradise (pepper) · deep-fried parsley leaves as garnish*

Cut the avocados in half, remove the stone and tease out the flesh. Mix the avocado flesh with the lemon juice and 2 tbsp. of olive oil in a mixer until creamy. Season with Fleur de Sel.

Cut the bread into 1/4 inch slices using a slicing machine. Then cut into 1 x 1 inch squares and roast in a frying pan without oil until crispy on both sides.

Cut the tuna into 1 1/2 inch wide strips. Roll the strips in the Grains of Paradise and briefly fry in olive oil. The tuna should remain raw. Cut the strips into 1/3 inch thick slices.

Spread the avocado mixture on the bread and add the tuna slices. Lightly salt with Fleur de Sel and garnish with the deep-fried parsley leaves.

Für die blauen Kartoffelchips hobelt man Trüffelkartoffeln in hauchdünne Scheiben, tupft sie mit Küchenpapier trocken und frittiert sie kurz in 175 Grad heißem Pflanzenöl.

The blue potato chips are made from wafer-thin slices of blue potato. Dry them slightly on a paper towel and briefly deep-fry at 350 °F in vegetable oil.

GEFÜLLTE MAISPOULARDENBRÜSTCHEN

Zutaten für 4 Personen: 4 Maispoulardenbrüste · 150 g süße Sahne · 35 g Wasabipaste (japanischer Meerrettich) · 1 Ei · Salz und Pfeffer · Muskatnuss · Butter für die Folie · frittierte Korianderblätter, Trüffelkartoffelchips und Pfeffersegel zum Garnieren

Aus den Maispoulardenbrüsten die Filets auslösen. Filets mit der Sahne, der Wasabipaste und dem Ei im Mixer zu einer Farce verarbeiten. Mit Salz, Pfeffer und Muskatnuss abschmecken.

Den Backofen auf 170 Grad vorheizen. In die Poulardenbrüste eine Tasche schneiden und die Farce einfüllen. 4 Alu-folienstücke, die etwas größer als die Poulardenbrüste sind, mit Butter einstreichen und die gefüllten Poulardenbrüste darauf-legen. Jedes Stück fest zusammenrollen. Im heißen Ofen ca. 15 Minuten garen.

Portionsweise auf den Linsen anrichten und mit frittierten Korianderblättern, Trüffelkartoffelchips sowie Pfeffersegeln garnieren.

LINSEN MIT KORIANDER

Zutaten für 4 Personen: 1 Karotte, fein gewürfelt · 1/2 Knollensellerie, fein gewürfelt · 1 weiße Zwiebel, fein ge-würfelt · 1 EL Olivenöl · 500 ml Gemüsebrühe · 100 g schwarze Linsen · 100 g gelbe Linsen · Fleur de Sel · Pfeffer · 1 TL Butter · 1 EL gehackter Koriander

Karotte, Sellerie und Zwiebel im Olivenöl anschwitzen. Mit der Gemüsebrühe ablöschen und die schwarzen Linsen zufügen. 20 Minuten köcheln lassen. Wenn die schwarzen Linsen fast gar sind, die gelben Linsen untermischen.

Die Linsen mit Fleur de Sel und Pfeffer abschmecken, die Butter und den Koriander unterziehen.

STUFFED CORN-FED CHICKEN BREAST

Ingredients for 4 people: *4 corn-fed chicken breasts · 5 fl. oz. single cream · 1 oz. wasabi paste (Japanese horseradish) · 1 egg · salt and pepper · nutmeg · butter · deep-fried coriander leaves, blue potato chips and pepper sails to garnish*

Tease out the filets from the chicken breasts. Mixer the filets, wasabi and egg into a paste. Season with salt, pepper and nutmeg.

Pre-heat the oven to 340 °F. Cut a pocket in the chicken breasts and fill with the paste. Butter 4 pieces of aluminum foil slightly larger than the chicken breasts and lay the chicken on them. Roll each one into a parcel and bake in the oven for around 15 minutes until done.

Arrange the chicken on a plate on top of the lentils and garnish with deep-fried coriander leaves, blue potato chips and pepper sails.

LENTILS WITH CORIANDER

Ingredients for 4 people: *1 carrot, finely diced · 1/2 bunch of celery, finely diced · 1 white onion, finely diced · 1 tbsp. olive oil · 2 cups vegetable stock · 3 1/2 oz. black lentils · 3 1/2 oz. yellow lentils · Fleur de Sel · pepper · 1 tsp. butter · 1 tsp. chopped coriander*

Sauté the carrots, celery and onion in olive oil. Pour in the stock and add the black lentils. Cook gently for 20 minutes. When the black lentils are almost done, stir in the yellow lentils.

Season the lentils with Fleur de Sel and pepper, fold in the butter and coriander.

Ein köstliches Dessert, das man sehr gut vorbereiten kann. Die harmonische Kombination von süßen und säuerlichen Geschmacksnoten wird Ihren Gästen lange in angenehmer Erinnerung bleiben.

This delicious dessert can be prepared in advance. It is a wonderfully harmonious combination of sweet and sour flavors that your guests will not forget.

MASCARPONE-EIS

Zutaten für 8 Personen: 500 ml Milch · 500 g süße Sahne · Mark von 1/2 Vanilleschote · 2 Eier · 2 Eigelb · 30 g Zucker · 150 g Mascarpone

Die Milch mit der Sahne und dem Vanillemark aufkochen. Eier, Eigelb und Zucker über dem heißen Wasserbad schaumig schlagen. Den Mascarpone einrühren und die Masse anschließend in der Eismaschine gefrieren lassen.

GEWÜRZKUCHEN AUF RHABARBER

Zutaten für 8 Personen: 250 g Butter · 360 g Zucker · 1 TL Lebkuchengewürz · 5 Eier · 5 Eigelb · 200 g flüssige Zartbitter-Kuvertüre · 160 g Mehl · 4 getrocknete Aprikosen, fein gewürfelt · 4 Backpflaumen, fein gewürfelt · Butter und Zucker für die Förmchen · 200 ml Weißwein · 100 ml Rote Bete Saft · 2 Stangen Rhabarber, in 5 cm lange Stifte geschnitten · Krokantstreusel und Minzeblätter zum Garnieren

Den Backofen auf 180 Grad vorheizen. Die Butter mit 160 g Zucker und dem Lebkuchengewürz schaumig aufschlagen. Nach und nach die Eier und das Eigelb unterrühren. Zuletzt die flüssige Kuvertüre unter Rühren in dünnem Strahl dazugießen.

Das Mehl sieben und unter den Teig rühren, dann die Trockenfrüchte untermischen. Eine Backform ausbuttern und mit Zucker ausstreuen. Den Teig einfüllen und glattstreichen. Im heißen Ofen 15 Minuten backen. Auf einem Kuchengitter auskühlen lassen und portionsweise aufschneiden.

Den restlichen Zucker in einem Topf karamellisieren lassen und mit Wein und Rote Bete Saft ablöschen. Auf die Hälfte zu einem Sirup einkochen. Den Rhabarber im Sirup gar ziehen lassen.

Gewürzkuchen auf dem Rhabarber anrichten und mit Krokantstreuseln bestreuen. Mit Mascarpone-Eis-Nocken und Minzeblättern garnieren.

MASCARPONE ICE CREAM

Ingredients for 8 people: *17 fl. oz. milk · 17 fl. oz. single cream · seeds from 1/2 a vanilla pod · 2 eggs · 2 egg yolks · 1 oz. sugar · 5 oz. mascarpone*

Bring the milk, cream and vanilla briefly to a boil. Beat the eggs, egg yolks and sugar in a double boiler until light and fluffy. Stir in the mascarpone and freeze the mixture in an ice-cream maker.

SPICE CAKES ON RHUBARB

Ingredients for 8 people: *8 oz. butter · 12 1/2 oz. sugar · 1 tbsp. gingerbread spice · 5 eggs · 5 egg yolks · 7 fl. oz. liquid dark chocolate couverture · 6 oz. flour · 4 dried apricots, finely diced · 4 dried plums, finely diced · butter and sugar for the baking dish · 7 fl. oz. white wine · 3 1/2 fl. oz. beetroot juice · 2 pieces of rhubarb, cut into 2 inch long sticks · chopped nut brittle and mint leaves to garnish*

Pre-heat the oven to 350 °F. Beat the butter, 6 oz. sugar and the gingerbread spice until light and fluffy. Gradually stir in the eggs and egg yolks. Slowly pour in the liquid chocolate, stirring constantly.

Sieve the flour and stir into the mixture, then add the dried fruit. Butter a baking dish and sprinkle with sugar. Pour in the mixture and smooth the surface. Bake in a hot oven for 15 minutes. Allow to cool on a rack, then cut to size.

Caramelize the rest of the sugar in a pan and add the wine and beetroot juice. Reduce by half into a syrup. Add the rhubarb and allow to steep until done.

Arrange the spice cakes on the rhubarb and sprinkle with the nut brittle. Garnish with dollops of mascarpone ice cream and mint leaves.

Die molekulare Küche liegt im Trend. Neben den klassischen Küchenwerkzeugen wie Kochlöffel, Topf und Pfanne braucht man dafür auch Utensilien, die bisher in einer Küche eher ungewöhnlich waren wie beispielsweise Pipetten.

Molecular gastronomy is in fashion. For this type of cooking you not only need the usual kitchen utensils such as wooden spoons, pots and pans, but also things you would not normally find in the kitchen, for example a pipette.

ROTBARBE AUF FENCHELGEMÜSE

Zutaten für 4 Personen: 3 Stängel Staudensellerie · 1 Fenchelknolle · 2 Frühlingszwiebeln · 8 kleine Rotbarbenfilets · Fleur de Sel · 2 EL Olivenöl · 1 Knoblauchzehe, halbiert · einige Thymianzweige · Salz und Pfeffer · Safran · 50 ml Weißwein · 2 cl Pernod · geräuchertes Paprikapulver · Wildkräuter zum Garnieren

Die Staudensellerie in kleine Rauten schneiden. Den Fenchel halbieren, den Strunk keilförmig ausschneiden und die Fenchelblätter ebenfalls in kleine Rauten schneiden. Die Frühlingszwiebeln schräg in Stifte schneiden.

Die Fischfilets mit Fleur de Sel würzen und auf der Hautseite im Olivenöl anbraten. Knoblauch und Thymian zufügen. Sobald die Haut knusprig ist, den Fisch aus der Pfanne nehmen und auf einen Teller setzen.

In der Fischpfanne das Gemüse leicht anbraten. Mit Salz und Pfeffer würzen, den Safran zufügen und kurz anrösten. Den Wein angießen und mit Pernod abschmecken. Den Sud auf die Hälfte einkochen lassen, dann abgießen.

Die Fischfilets mit Paprikapulver bestreuen und mit der Unterseite auf das Gemüse in der Pfanne setzen. Bei kleiner Hitze gar ziehen lassen.

Inzwischen den Sud in 4 Pipetten füllen. Den Fisch portionsweise auf dem Gemüse anrichten, die Pipetten in den Fisch stecken. Mit Wildkräutern garnieren.

RED MULLET ON FENNEL VEGETABLES

Ingredients for 4 people: *3 sticks of celery · 1 fennel · 2 spring onions · 8 small red mullet filets · Fleur de Sel · 2 tbsp. olive oil · 1 garlic clove, halved · a few twigs of thyme · salt and pepper · 1 1/2 fl. oz. white wine · 2/3 fl. oz. Pernod · smoked capsicum powder · saffron · wild herbs to garnish*

Cut the celery into small diamond shapes. Halve the fennel and cut out the wedge-shaped stem. Cut the fennel leaves into small diamond shapes. Cut the spring onions lengthways into sticks.

Season the fish filets with Fleur de Sel and fry on the skin side in olive oil. Add the thyme and garlic. As soon as the skin is crispy, remove from the pan and set aside.

Lightly fry the vegetables in the pan used for the fish. Season with salt and pepper, add the saffron and briefly fry. Pour in the white wine and season to taste with the Pernod. Allow the liquid to reduce by half, then drain.

Sprinkle the fish with the capsicum powder and place skin-side up on the vegetables. Reduce the heat and cook until done.

In the meantime fill the liquid into 4 pipettes. Arrange the fish on the vegetables in portions and stick the pipettes into the fish. Garnish with herbs.

In der molekularen Küche von Ferran Adrià spielen Reaktionen und Prozesse eine große Rolle. In seinem Restaurant El Bulli hat der kreative Küchenchef eine Reihe von Produkten für diese Form der Zubereitung entwickelt, die im Fachhandel erhältlich sind.

Reactions and processes play a role in Ferran Adrià's molecular kitchen. In his restaurant El Bulli, the creative head chef has developed a range of products for this type of cooking that are available in specialist stores.

FENCHELLUFT

Zutaten für 4 Personen: 1 Fenchelknolle, gewürfelt · 100 ml Milch · Salz · 1 TL Pernod · 3 g Lecite (Lecithin), Texturas Ferran Adrià

Den Fenchel in Milch und Wasser weich kochen. Anschließend mit dem Stabmixer pürieren und durch ein feines Haarsieb passieren. Mit Salz und Pernod abschmecken und das Lecithin mit dem Stabmixer einarbeiten.

TOMATENPRALINEN AUF SPARGEL

Zutaten für 4 Personen: 4 Tomaten · 12 grüne Spargelspitzen · Salz · einige Safranfäden · 200 ml Gemüsebrühe · 1 TL Champagner-Essig · Pfeffer · Zucker · 1 EL Butter · 400 g Frischkäse · 2 EL fein gehackte Kräuter · 1–2 TL Zitronensaft · 4 frittierte Basilikumblätter

Die Tomaten blanchieren und enthäuten. Am Stielansatz ein kleines, maximal 1,5 cm großes Loch ausschneiden und die Tomaten durch diese Öffnung vorsichtig entkernen. Die Spargelspitzen in kochendem Salzwasser blanchieren.

Die Safranfäden in der Gemüsebrühe und dem Essig aufkochen, mit Salz, Pfeffer und Zucker abschmecken und mit der Butter leicht abbinden.

Den Frischkäse mit den Kräutern vermischen, mit Salz, Pfeffer und Zitronensaft abschmecken und in einen Spritzbeutel füllen. Die Tomaten leicht erwärmen und mit dem Frischkäse füllen. Spargelspitzen portionsweise auf der Safransauce anrichten und die Tomatenpralinen darauf setzen. Mit Fenchelluft und frittiertem Basilikum garnieren.

FENNEL CLOUD

Ingredients for 4 people: *1 fennel, diced · 3 1/2 fl. oz. milk · salt · 1 tsp. Pernod · 0.1 oz. Lecite (lecithin), Texturas Ferran Adrià*

Cook the fennel in milk and water until soft. Blend into a puree and press through a fine sieve. Season to taste with salt and Pernod, stir in the lecithin using a hand mixer.

TOMATO CANDIES ON ASPARAGUS

Ingredients for 4 people: *4 tomatoes · 12 green asparagus tips · salt · a few saffron threads · 3/4 cup vegetable stock · 1 tsp. champagne vinegar · pepper · sugar · 1 tbsp. butter · 14 oz. cream cheese · 2 tbsp. finely chopped herbs · 1–2 tsp. lemon juice · 4 deep-fried basil leaves*

Blanch and peel the tomatoes. Make a small hole, maximum of 1/2 inch, in the top of each tomato and carefully de-seed through the hole. Blanch the asparagus in boiling salted water.

Bring the vegetable stock, with the saffron and vinegar, briefly to a boil. Season to taste with salt, pepper and sugar and thicken slightly with the butter.

Mix the cream cheese and herbs together, season to taste with salt, pepper and lemon juice. Pour into a piping bag. Lightly warm the tomatoes and fill with the cream cheese. Arrange the asparagus tips on the saffron sauce and place the tomatoes on top. Garnish with fennel cloud and basil leaves.

Danksagung

Mein besonderer Dank gilt meinem Verleger Hendrik teNeues, der mich nicht nur zu diesem Buch ermuntert hat, sondern mich auch tatkräftig bei diesem Vorhaben unterstützte.

Ein großes Dankeschön geht an Uschi Capelle für die Leihgaben von Geschirr und Besteck aus ihrem Geschäft. Ebenso danke ich der Kofler & Kompanie AG für ihre tatkräftige Unterstützung mit Rezepten und für die Zubereitung der Gerichte für das Fotoshooting.

Bedanken möchte ich mich bei den Firmen Poggenpohl und Gaggenau, zwei renommierten Herstellern von hochwertigen Küchenausstattungen und innovativen Küchengeräten. Das intelligente Konzept, mit dem sie die Küche der Kofler & Kompanie AG eingerichtet haben, hat das Kochen zum Vergnügen gemacht.

Herzlichen Dank auch meinen Schlossgeistern, die bei der Vorbereitung der Tische geholfen haben. Und natürlich Carsten Sander für seine stimmungsvollen Fotos und Ingeborg Pils für ihre Texte.

Acknowledgements

Special thanks to my publisher Hendrik teNeues, who not only encouraged me to write this book, but also actively supported me in its creation.

A sincere thank you goes to Uschi Capelle for the loan of dinnerware and flatware from her store. Thanks also to Kofler & Kompanie AG for their energetic help with recipes and for the preparation of the food for the photo shoot.

I'd like to thank two highly reputed companies, Poggenpohl and Gaggenau, for their quality kitchen fixtures and equipment. The intelligent concept they developed for the kitchen, together with Kofler & Kompanie AG, made cooking a pleasure.

Thanks also to my friendly house-hold staff, who helped me prepare the table decorations, to Carsten Sander for his breathtaking photography and Ingeborg Pils for her wonderful text.

Stephanie Gräfin Bruges von Pfuel wurde 1961 in München geboren.
Nach dem Studium an der Universität für Bodenkultur in Wien arbeitete die diplomierte Forstingenieurin zunächst als Angestellte im land- und forstwirtschaftlichen Betrieb ihres Vaters, Karl Freiherr Michel von Tüßling.
1991 erbte sie nach dem Tod ihres Vaters den gesamten Familienbesitz, zu dem neben 1100 Hektar Wald auch ein baufälliges Schloss aus dem 16. Jahrhundert gehörte. 1992 begann Stephanie Gräfin Bruges von Pfuel mit den umfangreichen Renovierungs- und Sanierungsarbeiten, die bis heute andauern.
Inzwischen zählt Tüßling zu den schönsten und am besten erhaltenen Renaissanceschlössern Bayerns. Der Barocksaal und andere Räumlichkeiten werden für Feste und Events vermietet, um zumindest einen Teil der laufenden Renovierungskosten zu finanzieren. Seit 2003 finden im Schlosspark jährlich die Tüßlinger Gartentage statt, im Herbst 2008 erstmals das Festival Bella Vita. Doch nicht nur geschäftlich, auch privat ist die Schlossherrin gerne und mit viel Hingabe Gastgeberin. Ihre fröhlichen, fantasievollen und dennoch bodenständigen Tischdekorationen sind weithin bekannt.
Stephanie Gräfin Bruges von Pfuel ist so vielseitig wie ihr wunderschönes Schloss, das sie mit ihren sechs Kindern bewohnt. Die erfolgreiche Unternehmerin und Mutter ist Mitglied des Marktgemeinderats Tüßling, Ehrenrichterin am Sozialgericht München sowie Mitglied des Ausschusses des bayerischen Waldbesitzerverbandes und des Beirats des bayerischen Grundbesitzerverbandes. Darüber hinaus engagiert sie sich für SOS-Kinderdörfer und ist deren Botschafterin und Repräsentantin.

Carsten Sander ist bekannt für seine meisterhaft inszenierten Bildwelten. Er beschäftigt sich hauptsächlich mit Menschen, gerne auch mit Prominenten. Der Fotokünstler lebt in Berlin und Düsseldorf und arbeitet weltweit. Mit diesem Buch unternimmt er erstmals einen Ausflug in die Interior- und Food-Fotografie.

Stephanie Gräfin Bruges von Pfuel was born in 1961 in Munich.
On completion of her academic studies at the Universität für Bodenkultur in Vienna she worked as a graduate forestry engineer in her father's agriculture and forestry company.
In 1991, following the death of her father (Karl Freiherr Michel von Tüßling) she inherited the family estate including 1,100 hectares of forest and a dilapidated 16th century manor-house. Stephanie Gräfin Bruges von Pfuel began with the extensive renovation and refurbishment of the house in 1992, work that is still going on today.
Schloss Tüßling is now one of the most beautiful and best-kept renaissance houses in Bavaria. The baroque hall and other areas are available for parties and events. This helps to finance at least part of the renovation costs. Since 2003 the yearly Tüßling garden show has taken place in the grounds and in 2008 the Bella Vita festival was held there for the first time. The countess is a dedicated hostess of commercial events as well as ones for private occasions. Her bright, imaginative and yet down-to-earth table decorations are widely known.
Stephanie Gräfin Bruges von Pfuel is as multifaceted as the wonderful manor-house in which she lives with her six children. She is a successful businesswoman and mother, a member of the Tüßling community council, a lay judge for the Social Court in Munich and a committee member of the Bavarian forest-owners' association and advisory committee member of the Bavarian landowners' association. She is also actively supportive of the SOS-Kinderdorf charity as well as being their ambassador and representative.

Carsten Sander is renowned for his beautifully arranged visual creations. He is mainly engaged in photographing people, including celebrities. The photographer practices his art worldwide and lives in Berlin and Düsseldorf. This book is his first foray into interior and food photography.

Bezugsquellen / Resources

Kofler & Kompanie AG
International Caterer
Unter den Linden 2
D-10117 Berlin
Telefon +49 - (0) 30 - 25 92 89 - 0 | Fax: -11
berlin@koflerkompanie.com
www.koflerkompanie.com

Haus und Garten
Bahnhofstraße 36
D-84524 Neuötting
Telefon +49 - (0) 8671 - 20152
hcapelle@gmx.de

Gaggenau Hausgeräte GmbH
Carl-Wery-Straße 34
D-81739 München
www.gaggenau.com

Poggenpohl Möbelwerke GmbH
Poggenpohlstraße 1
D-32051 Herford
www.poggenpohl.de

Das Einhorn im Garten
Lauterbachstraße 10
D-80997 München
gabriele.von.liel@t-online.de
www.daseinhornimgarten.de

© 2008 teNeues Verlag GmbH + Co. KG, Kempen

Edited by Stephanie von Pfuel
Produced by ditter.projektagentur GmbH
Texts by Stephanie von Pfuel, Ingeborg Pils
Photographs by Carsten Sander
Recipes by Kofler & Kompanie AG
Food for Photography by Kofler & Kompanie AG
Design and Layout by Ilona Buchholz
Editorial Assistance by Julia Sodomann
Translation by Daniela Thoma for Equipo de Edición
Color separation by Klaussner Medien Service GmbH

Published by teNeues Publishing Group

teNeues Verlag GmbH + Co. KG
Am Selder 37, 47906 Kempen, Germany
Tel 0049-(0)2152-916-0, Fax 0049-(0)2152-916-111
e-mail: books@teneues.de

Press department: Andrea Rehn
Tel 0049-(0)2152-916-202
e-mail: arehn@teneues.de

teNeues Publishing Company
16 West 22nd Street, New York, N.Y. 10010, USA
Tel 001-212-627-9090, Fax 001-212-627-9511

teNeues Publishing UK Ltd.
P.O. Box 402, West Byfleet, KT14 7ZF, Great Britain
Tel 0044-1932-4035-09, Fax 0044-1932-4035-14

teNeues France S.A.R.L.
93, rue Bannier, 45000 Orléans, France
Tel 0033-2-3854-1071, Fax 0033-2-3862-5340

www.teneues.com

ISBN 978-3-8327-9273-2

Printed in Italy

Bibliographic information published by Die Deutsche Bibliothek.
Die Deutsche Bibliothek lists this publication in the Deutsche Nationalbibliografie;
detailed bibliographic data is available in the Internet at http://dnb.ddb.de.